French
Flair

French
Flair
CREATING A HOME INSPIRED
BY FRENCH STYLE

FIFI O'NEILL

Photography by
MARK LOHMAN

CICO BOOKS

In memory of David Peters

Senior designer Toni Kay
Editor Sophie Devlin
Production manager Gordana Simakovic
Senior commissioning editor Annabel Morgan
Art director Sally Powell
Creative director Leslie Harrington

Published in 2025 by Ryland Peters & Small
20–21 Jockey's Fields
London WC1R 4BW
and
1452 Davis Bugg Road
Warrenton, NC 27589
www.rylandpeters.com
email: euregulations@rylandpeters.com

Text copyright © Fifi O'Neill 2025
Design and photography copyright
© CICO Books 2025

10 9 8 7 6 5 4 3 2 1

ISBN 978-1-80065-417-4

A CIP record for this book is available
from the British Library.

Library of Congress CIP data
has been applied for.

Printed and bound in China

The authorised representative in the EEA
is Authorised Rep Compliance Ltd.,
Ground Floor, 71 Lower Baggot Street,
Dublin, D02 P593, Ireland
www.arccompliance.com

FSC
www.fsc.org
MIX
Paper | Supporting
responsible forestry
FSC® C106563

Contents

Introduction

"What is done in love is done well."
VINCENT VAN GOGH

What is "French Flair"? It's an instinctive ability to strike a balance between the elegant and the unexpected. It's that indefinable, elusive, pleasing quality the French call *je ne sais quoi*. And when it comes to interiors, French Flair always finds its center, no matter how many disparate elements you throw into the mix—from old-world sensibility to modern sophistication.

In French-inspired interiors, design and lifestyle play equal roles. Spaces boast an easy sophistication because they are never too curated or too perfect. Contemporary art stands alongside century-old paintings, modern accessories rest on antique furniture and rustic elements are juxtaposed with novel amenities, yet it all fits together coherently and harmoniously. The distinctive and versatile aesthetic appears effortless because its fundamental principle is rooted in comfort and individuality.

Another major component of French Flair is *l'art de vivre*, which is all about making daily routines special—from enjoying meals outdoors to putting fresh flowers in every room or picking up herbs and vegetables from the potager.

Though the homes featured in this book embrace various facets of French decorating style, they share the same design philosophy that stems from the marriage of beauty with practicality and exude a welcome that is both warm and personal. That's the timeless magic of French Flair.

THE ELEMENTS

Simply Stylish Furnishings

In a French-inspired home, furniture is shapely and well scaled, with an eye toward balance. Its appearance is not beholden to one period; instead it freely mixes pedigree and provenance. Many pieces feature raw or distressed wood. Finding the perfect finish—whether faded paint on a table or the slightly tarnished gilding of a sconce—is part of creating a truly personal home. Look out for unique pieces with interesting details such as carving and scalloped edges, too.

The soft pink velvet of an antique chair marries perfectly with the gentle patina of a Swedish desk (opposite). In this bedroom, contrasting textures and materials work in harmony (above). The delicate bedding tempers the weathered finish of the vintage iron bed, while porcelain plates on the wall and sheer drapes hanging from a zinc canopy impart a sense of refinement. Incorporating a pair of wooden shutters keeps the more sophisticated elements down to earth. Carved by hand from mahogany and refinished in a subtle antique white, a French flea-market find is reborn as a display cabinet (right).

One hallmark of French interiors is that they never look too perfect. Beauty stems from the character of pieces rather than their grand lineage. Furniture may be streamlined, like this modest cabinet with a slightly rustic finish (above left), or highly decorative, such as this ample mirrored armoire with a cornice motif and intricate carvings (above). Many of the homes in this book incorporate a mix of aged antiques with low-key contemporary pieces (left and opposite). French Flair reflects an appreciation of various eras and designs, resulting in a timeless elegance with the beauty of a pared-down, organic approach.

Textural Finishes

Walls are often cloaked in plaster, stucco, stone or a blend of all three. If you choose simply to paint the walls, consider a glaze or other decorative treatment that will keep them from feeling flat. For the floors, slate, limestone, tiles and natural wood all strike the right notes.

Interiors that draw inspiration from the charm of the French countryside have a warm, inviting atmosphere while contributing to the overall aesthetic appeal of a space (opposite, above and right). Natural materials showcase specific textures that are equally at home inside as they are outside. Their irregular surfaces and colors complement classic lines and soft palettes. Wood, brick, stone and plaster walls, exposed beams overhead and slate and tiled floors are integral elements that offer versatility, functionality and character. While some may be painted, others are left in their original finish.

Wood flooring is an ideal complement to furniture with similar textures and tones, as seen in this dining room (below). The mismatched chairs are a fitting and whimsical addition to a humble farm table with chippy paintwork and a simple utilitarian étagère. Tumbled cement pavers make for a strong contrast with a sleek bathtub (right). From walkways to façades, substantial stone, brick and stucco are proudly exposed (below right).

A pristine palette needs distinctive items to keep it from being sterile. In this bathroom, a beam with a curvy chandelier, a gilded mirror and a vintage ladder are the perfect finishing touches.

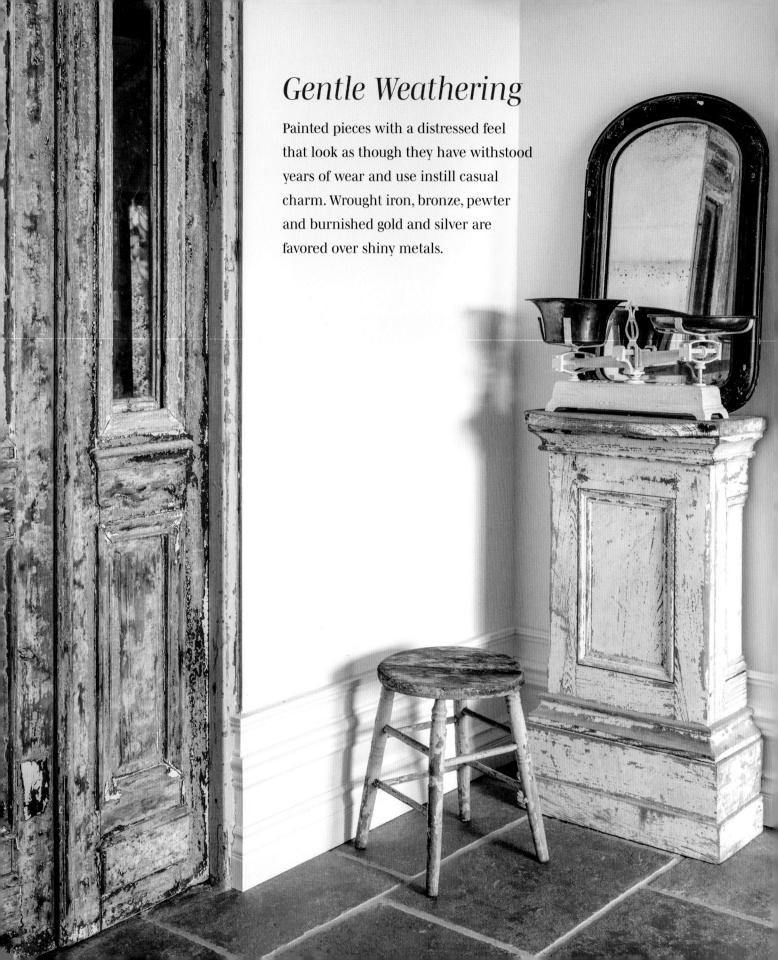

Gentle Weathering

Painted pieces with a distressed feel
that look as though they have withstood
years of wear and use instill casual
charm. Wrought iron, bronze, pewter
and burnished gold and silver are
favored over shiny metals.

When it comes to honoring the passage of time, including pieces that show a charmingly aged look is one of France's favorite interior decorating features. Their worn appearance and idiosyncratic character speak of their past lives through their imperfections, natural mellowing and gentle decay. In typical French fashion, architectural remnants are often given a new function (opposite). Silver domes, urns and weathered furniture may also play a starring role (above, above right and right). Whether in a new or period home, their presence defines the French aesthetic.

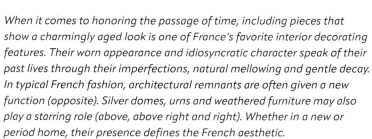

Grouping objects and furniture of similar values creates visual interest and establishes the mood of a space, whether sophisticated, rustic or casual (opposite). Accessories are the indispensable touches that bring a room together, as shown in these photographs (right). A classical bust and sculpted hand reflect a sense of history and artistry. Heart-shaped carvings and a stone garden cherub have sentimental value. A weatherworn chair and flower bucket look as though they were made for each other. Old leather-bound tomes, a vintage still-life painting and a gilded mirror recall the faded grandeur of the past.

Fabrics and Textiles

From the famed silks of Lyon to classic toiles
de Jouy and the mille-fleurs prints of Provence,
many fabrics speak French with just the right
accent. Natural linen and cotton have tactile
interest and a relaxed feel. Include a few notes
of gingham, stripes and florals with
plains for a pleasing mélange.

French Flair's enviable blend of charm and simplicity is the height of domestic chic. Thanks to their exceptional quality, elegant designs and history-laden production methods, French fabrics have long been iconic favorites. From traditional blue-and-white florals to bold stripes, the patterned possibilities are numerous (opposite). Texture is just as important: French-inspired textiles encompass fine silks and homespun linens, delicate sheers and embroidered designs (above left, above and left). Consider pairing rustic upholstery or relaxed bed linens with elegant tapestries or delicate lace.

To bring a French accent to a new kitchen, a panel salvaged from an antique floor screen has been repurposed into a rack to create a stylish display and keep handy a collection of pretty yet functional dish towels (below). Drying lavender and fresh garden roses add to the charming country feel.

Traditional ticking, classic toile and sturdy flax are just the right touches for a rustic bedroom complete with an organic twig wreath and weathered accessories (opposite). Antique chairs can be updated with a ruffled trim or reupholstered with grain sack fabric, demonstrating the remarkable versatility of French fabrics on new or old furniture (top). A hand-embroidered linen pouf with silk tassels from Morocco—once a French protectorate— instills a touch of history and global flavor (above left). Fashioned into a valance/pelmet, a tapestry remnant confers a regal touch on a vintage home (above).

Color Palettes

French-inspired hues have a gentleness that translates into instant comfort. Whites are warm and have layered depth—think cream, ecru, ivory or oatmeal. Grays are smoky, silvery and muted. Other colors draw from the landscape: dusky sage and lavender, sunny yellow and sky blue, peony pink and touches of red. Above all, harmony is the key.

Against a backdrop featuring neutral and textural elements, a single color brings a clean, vibrant note that enhances the purity of the space (opposite). Rosy pink and soft gray accents set a tender and sophisticated mood (above). In this living room, a harmonious atmosphere stems from the integration of the chair's charcoal velvet upholstery with textural accessories in a variety of brown tones (right). The colors of a cotton hand-block-printed throw recall those of the pink flowers on the side table.

ARRÊT
COUR

59

A neutral gray palette is warmed by decorative accessories in similar tonal hues (opposite). Blues—from powdery shades to brilliant azure, indigo, inky tones and more—together with crisp and hushed whites are a classic color pairing of French interiors. Favored for its enduring appeal, the much-loved combination can be seen here in countless variations on the theme (right). From a single enamel pitcher to pillows with a floral pattern, a painted clock, kitchen decor, wallpaper and a vintage cabinet, blue and white are always on trend.

Displays With Purpose

Rarely will collected objects be purely decorative. They usually have an undertone of usefulness: wall-hung plates within easy reach for service, pitchers and jars that house kitchen staples and baskets that corral garden produce. Open shelving is a natural fit for this look—everyday items enjoy pride of place rather than languishing behind cabinet doors.

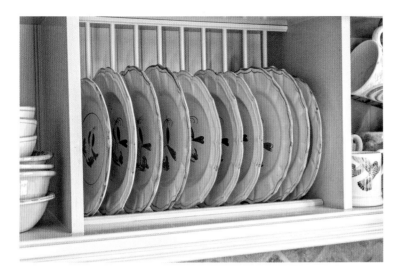

Items do not have to be part of a set. What matters is how they function within your daily life and how they can make chores more enjoyable. In a small eating area, everyday glassware lines the shelves of a vintage cabinet in French-restaurant style (below left). Cabinets outfitted with chicken wire allow collections of ironstone dishes to be seen (below). Platters and plates in a symmetrical display complement those in the cupboards. Everything has a place, a purpose and a decorative value.

The French have a way of elevating even the most utilitarian items by making them part of the decor in unique ways. An old crate becomes a tray, while an urn makes a perfectly proper silverware container (opposite). A plate rack keeps dishes on hand with a pleasing aesthetic (above).

Creating a useful and appealing display in the kitchen comes down to selecting items with shapes, dimensions and colors that contribute to a cohesive look. Here, gold and glass accents set off white dishes and sculptural items (above). A floor-to ceiling built-in plate rack acts as a jewel box for silverware (opposite).

Floral Flair

The French are all about flowers, which overflow the sidewalk markets of Paris, burst brilliant poppy red along rural roadsides and turn the countryside fragrant in lovely rows of lavender. It's no wonder that French homes rely on fresh blooms, from dainty sprigs to lavish bouquets and potted herbs, to impart a living element to their rooms.

In France, selecting flowers is akin to choosing the perfect baguette hot from the oven. The quintessential bread not only has to be golden and crunchy, it also has to smell delicious. Similarly, flowers must have the right appearance, texture, color and fragrance. French market stalls and flower shops always offer what is in season. You don't need many blooms to make a room come alive (opposite). However, the manner in which they are arranged or planted is very much part of the mood they impart, as these indoor and outdoor spaces reveal (left, below left and below).

When it comes to containers and types of arrangements, there is no rule. Planters, bottles, buckets and vessels intended for all other purposes are put into service with results as surprising as they are beautiful. Here we see a variety of effortless displays: succulents sprouting out of a concrete head, a single stem of hibiscus in a glass bottle and a showy agapanthus standing tall in an old zinc bucket (left, right and below).

A vintage porcelain footed vase with a hand-painted finish heightens the opulence of an array of lush garden roses. The sumptuous pink and white blossoms have abundant layers upon layers of petals for a lavishly romantic display.

Finishing Touches

It only takes a little accessorizing to make a room special, uniquely yours and feel collected, not contrived. Imagine piles of books casually displayed, mismatched candlesticks, family treasures, souvenirs from travels abroad, evocative signs, personal collections and eclectic groupings of art, all presented without overthinking their placement.

Whether your taste favors antiques, art or mementoes, introducing items that easily straddle the line of sophisticated and simple, elegant and rustic is always a good approach (opposite and above). Keep your displays interesting and grounded with hints of gold, patina, natural texture and organic pieces.

Grouped into a theme, like this parade of antique clockfaces, a collection becomes more than just an interesting vignette (above). It signifies a personal connection with history. A clear vase filled with apples and hydrangeas makes a fresh, verdant accessory (left). A grand, ornate antique clock contributes its singular visual beauty and an elegant counterpoint to the modernity of the steel doors on either side (opposite). It proves that accessorizing well is about composition and balance.

Creative Reuse

"Plus ça change, plus c'est la même chose": The more things change, goes the old epigram by French writer Jean-Baptiste Alphonse Karr, the more they stay the same. *Les Français* embrace the sustainable, eco-friendly philosophy of reinventing and repurposing decorative elements. To achieve this sought-after aesthetic, they practice the art of *chiner* (scouring flea markets, antiques shops and garage sales).

Brocantes, vide-greniers and braderies are the most-loved outlets in France where you can find unique objects and furniture to reinvent. Large or small, pristine or weathered, items passed on from one generation to the next pair well with those collected over time from these flea markets. Here we see a whimsical birdcage, old books and sculptural stone angels reborn into imaginative decorating elements (opposite and above).

Vintage fabrics, in particular monogrammed ones and those with delicate trims, are prized for their elegance. These examples have been made into decorative pillowcases and coverlets and paired with an antique daybed repurposed as a sofa (left). Antique shutters offer a clever and unexpected showcase for a beautiful marriage of flea-market finds (below left). Though they originated from different brocantes and feature disparate materials and finishes, a gilded mirror, silver Champagne bucket and a garden cherub are unified by their romantic theme (below).

Previously fitted with a mirror, a hand-carved frame has been given a pretty but practical function as a chalkboard (opposite). Pairing it with a small, narrow bench topped with blue hydrangeas in a zinc garden planter creates an interesting and visually pleasing composition.

THE HOMES

1

L'Art de Vivre

ABOVE *A grouping composed of a vintage painting from a Paris flea market, a cast-aluminum plaque from 1939 and an engraved ironstone crock complements the kitchen's French charm.*

RIGHT *In the entryway, varied materials and a mix of finishes and textures play well together. Sleek iron and glass doors are tempered with slender vintage shutters, while a pine buffet and an old bucket add warmth to the stone floor.*

Maison du
Cheval Noir

OPPOSITE *A handcrafted marble sink exemplifies timeless style with its perfectly aged surface. It is supported by a pair of rustic wooden posts with a carved decorative border that frames a grain sack curtain—a stylish way to conceal kitchen necessities.*

Elfin Forest—the name alone conjures up a magical realm. But if that wasn't enough to intrigue you, the home of Andalynn and Brandon Richie is sure to bewitch you. Picture yourself surrounded by an abundance of luscious, fragrant roses and aromatic lavender as you pause to revel in their heady scent. Look up and take in the beauty of the house set high above the terraced gardens, then as if someone just waved a magic wand, you find yourself in the South of France. But, au contraire, you are in Southern California and this enchanting setting is wondrously real.

THIS PAGE & ABOVE RIGHT *In the kitchen, old-world heritage meshes beautifully with function. "The niche trimmed with vintage timbers was created to accommodate the range and a large vent hood," Andalynn explains. Copper pots, French signage and old wooden cutting boards add authentic and aesthetically pleasing touches.*

W HEN THE RICHIES ACQUIRED THE PROPERTY in 2012, it held no resemblance to its current and undeniably French elegance. "My dear friend Gail found this house for us," Andalynn recalls. "Though there was absolutely nothing appealing about it, she knew it could be amazing. What called to us was the potential it held."

Of special interest to Andalynn, who loves horses, was the land that surrounds the house. "It was perfect to build barns, riding facilities and gardens. I loved that it was just asking to be terraced with stone walls and rose and lavender borders." Today the stables and pastures are home to 30 horses. In fact, she has renamed the property Maison du Cheval Noir in honor of one in particular, which she describes as her "heart horse."

Andalynn's significant design background and her experience working with historic homes and antiques proved invaluable to the metamorphosis of the original nondescript property, which was built in 1980. "I started working for my family's commercial design and construction company when I was 13, first in the design library and then I moved into the furniture showroom and art gallery," she explains. "I learned to draft and do color boards, and I also studied design in college."

The kitchen is a fusion of elegance and informality. Vaulted ceilings and ample arched doors were incorporated to add dimension and light. Andalynn designed the marble-topped pine islands to replicate classic French butchers' tables. Their scalloped detail echoes the trim under the sink. She is fond of time-honored styles and created a custom shelving display that recalls the interiors of Parisian restaurants.

ABOVE & LEFT *The textures and hues of the dining room's limestone wall and fireplace create a neutral backdrop for black iron sconces and matching doors. Antique chairs have been upholstered in dark blue and olive green silk. The white oak table and hutch/dresser maintain the sophisticated color scheme. Antique figurines speak of Andalynn's bond with horses.*

French architecture and furnishings have long been favorites, but Andalynn also buys items from all over Europe, including the UK, Italy and Sweden. "There was nothing French about the original structure of the house," she recalls. "We altered the rooflines, installed new windows and doors, reconfigured the turret entry and added French gates outside. It changed everything." Cladding the exterior in a custom color stucco in a semi-smooth Santa Barbara finish and limestone also contributed to the home's French country allure.

For the interiors, Andalynn envisioned a farmhouse aesthetic, not too formal or stuffy. "I manifested it one room at a time and relied on what I saw when I looked at a space. I also allowed the house to be what it wanted to be—I believe nothing in design should be forced or contrived." Another influential element was the desire to incorporate furniture she had already purchased.

With beautifully rendered artisanal, earthy materials and an appreciation of fine craftsmanship, Andalynn masterfully extols the best of French farmhouse style.

"I love the way the pieces in each room communicate with each other."

The living room has a subdued palette of whites and pale colors, which reflects the natural light streaming through the glazed doors. A black piano from 1880 anchors the space and provides contrast and depth for the layering of European antique furnishings and accessories.

ABOVE *Because the guest bedroom is where Andalynn's daughters stay when they come to visit, it has a feminine flair. The walls are painted in the palest shade of pink attained from mixing Calamine and All White, both from Farrow & Ball. The bed's black canopy frame, curtain rods and windows provide a sophisticated element in contrast with the pink and white bed linens.*

From one space to the next, the integrity of the materials imparts authenticity. "Reclaimed limestone and marble fireplaces, salvaged beams and doors, and stone floors and the like give the space the illusion that it has been here for centuries, and that authenticity is important to me." She adds, "Not everything has to be old, but I couldn't imagine designing a home and picking items from a catalog. That would seem very soulless to me."

As for the garden, the couple started from scratch to create layers of landscaping and a profusion of flowers. It began with building stone walls to create multilevel terraces and outdoor rooms. "The only plants that are original to the property are the olive trees, a few fruit trees and a giant magnolia," Andalynn explains.

OPPOSITE *Andalynn added an antique Victorian pitch pine mantel embellished with gesso carvings to the guest bedroom fireplace. Acquired in Paris, favorite artwork depicting French scenes is given pride of place. A pair of antique chairs upholstered in vintage pink velvet underscores the room's gentle ambience. Old books are set atop a perfectly distressed 1900s footstool.*

Beauty and function come together in the simple yet elegant bathroom. A French mirror and a pair of sconces from a Paris flea market stand above an antique sideboard fitted with a marble top, a stone sink and original hardware. Cement tiles ground the room while adding another level of texture to the neutral palette.

RIGHT *Details matter to Andalynn's approach. Here, a patinated cast-iron soap dish offers a spot for fresh flowers, a staple of French interiors.*

BELOW *Tiles in gray and white continue the calm, sophisticated mood of the bathroom. The freestanding tub, glass shelves and silver accessories impart a luxurious spa-like atmosphere, with the period-style fittings recalling vintage elements found in French hotels.*

"I have planted everything else myself, including more than 200 roses (and counting) and the lavender borders."

When asked if she has a favorite item in the house, Andalynn is quick to answer: "I can't pick one. I adore French mirrors and my Swedish clock and my square grand piano, but most of all I love the way the pieces in each room communicate with each other." The same applies to the rooms of the house. "It's like asking to choose a favorite child—I love them all!"

ABOVE *In the traditional French lifestyle, living takes place outside as often as inside. Andalynn has embraced this philosophy and made the outdoor spaces feel comfortable and inviting.*

LEFT *Defined by gravel paths and verdant edgings, fragrant rose beds of all sizes and a variety of aromatic plantings abound all through the property. Each of these peaceful, restorative and perfumed areas is beneficial to humans and birds alike.*

RIGHT *With its time-honored architecture, stone façade, iron gates and wooden shutters, the Richies' home is equally fit for the French countryside as for its California location.*

OPPOSITE *An antique chandelier from a French flea market presides over an armchair that had been used as a movie prop and was destined for the dumpster/skip. "It was in great condition, so I brought it home and had it reupholstered in linen," Angela says.*

ABOVE & RIGHT *A sumptuous floral arrangement springs from a vintage French cheese box. Elsewhere, Angela has paired thrifted pieces such as a Louis XVI vanity and French cane chair with a glamorous mirror from a Beverly Hills estate sale.*

A Feast
for the Senses

Angela Mann once outfitted brides for their big day. Now, she dresses her California home with a similar goal in mind—to make her rooms beautiful, elegant and memorable. "My work has always been artistic in some way, whether it was designing, sewing, painting or creating flower arrangements for clients and also for myself," says Angela, who graduated from the Fashion Institute of Design & Merchandising and worked as an independent designer for many years.

TODAY, AS A SCENIC ARTIST AND PAINTER in the movie industry, Angela's expertise is in high demand. "I love my work," she says. "It's very creative and changes constantly. I find it fulfilling and rewarding."

There is a quiet sense of refinement in her Los Angeles home, where her love of vintage is always underscored by lavish bouquets spilling out from unique vessels. "I grew up surrounded by flowers," she recalls. "My mother had the most amazing garden. The scent of her roses and lilacs still lingers in my memory." Even as a child, Angela was always making whimsical little bouquets. "Every time we went on a road trip with my family, my dad would pull over to the side of the road where wildflowers grew and let me pick an armful."

Angela now has her own garden, a floral oasis from where bountiful blooms become an intrinsic design element of her home. "It's my therapy and my happiness," she says. "I am so content when I am surrounded by flowers. They make me feel connected to nature and remind me of the simple pleasures of life."

Angela's sense of style is evident not only in her floral artistry but also in the containers she chooses to show them at their best. One-of-a-kind vessels—from urns to jardinières, Champagne buckets and more—play a major role. "I've been collecting unique items to be used as vases for as long as I can remember," she says. "I look for those with patina and age, and I especially love cast iron or anything gilded. I find so many gorgeous pieces at flea markets and estate sales. Anything that says French or European will most likely come home with me."

Though she says it's hard to pinpoint where her fondness of the French aesthetic that imbues her home comes from, she offers a fanciful possibility. "I've been told many times that I might have been a French woman in a past life! But seriously, I adore French interiors for their timeless elegance and sophistication. They exude warmth, refinement and romance. It's a way of life that celebrates beauty, sophistication and the art of living well."

Upon moving into her current home, Angela quickly began to add her own flair to the rooms. "My style is simple, elegant and eclectic at the same time," she explains. "I like mixing new, antique and vintage pieces. Collectively, they create a warm and inviting atmosphere with touches of the past while keeping things fresh and current." To evoke a lived-in yet refined ambience, she chose to paint the walls in Chantilly Lace by Benjamin Moore "to allow the furnishings, art and accessories to be the focal points."

In the open-plan living and dining room, similar fabrics and wood tones with white, ebonized or black accents create a sense of cohesion. Angela's favorite space is the dining area. "Some of my most cherished items are there, including lots of unmatched French china collected throughout the years." It makes her happy to surround herself with all things beautiful and meaningful. "I only purchase items that I fall in love with, and I proudly display and include them in my everyday life," she says. "The dining area is also the gathering place for family and friends. I love sharing meals around the table."

PAGES 66 & 67 *Colorful flowers brighten Angela's garden. In the breakfast area, she skillfully mixes old and new. In lieu of a tray, a large antique mirror holds a garden cherub and a vintage silver bucket on a new table, while a newly constructed plate rack (a weekend project) displays some of Angela's prized collection of silver.*

ABOVE *The new kitchen is Angela's domain. "I can spend hours making up with my own recipes," she explains. "My inner Julia Child comes out when I start using all my French copper cookware."*

RIGHT *Angela's affinity for art, portraits and landscapes in particular is front and center in the vignettes she creates in every room. In the dining room, a marble sculpture stands by an oil portrait of a child.*

"I've been told many times that I might have been a French woman in a past life!"

PAGE 69 Angela's favorite piece is the dining-room chandelier. "It was used on a TV set I worked on," she explains. "At the end of the show, it was given to me!" Gold and black accents add depth and warmth to the room, while antiques balance the cool modernity of the marble table.

ABOVE "I have been looking for an armoire that could function as a bar and display my vintage etched wineglasses and mismatched French porcelain dishes that I've been collecting forever," says Angela. For now, she has opted for a new French casement cabinet to house her collections.

The living room is another example of Angela's ability to seamlessly create stylish yet affordable spaces. A new slipcovered sofa, French-style chairs upholstered in charcoal velvet and a glass and brass table take on a classic demeanor when united with vintage artwork, mirrors and lamps.

BELOW *The en-suite bathroom has been remodeled with a marble-topped vanity that matches the walls. New mirrors, a vintage chandelier and a pair of wall lights give the space a sophisticated appeal. An exquisite hand-painted porcelain and cast-iron French urn overflows with garden roses.*

RIGHT *"I believe every room should have a French armoire," says Angela. She is also partial to gilding and has highlighted the intricate carvings of this example in the bedroom with touches of gold. She also applied gold leaf to a formerly brown flea-market chair to complete the look.*

Elegant fabrics and carved furnishings speak French in every room, while gilded touches, mirrors and chandeliers lend their own fancy flourishes and visual strength, and create a sense of opulence and refinement.

Clearly, Angela's inner French woman is well and alive in her home. "I say this all the time— as long as you have a large gilded French mirror, a sparkly chandelier and a beautiful vase full of garden roses, your room is pretty much done!"

"I wanted the bedroom to be a little masculine and a little feminine at the same time," Angela explains. She achieved her goal by toning down refined pieces such as the Empire chandelier and vintage sconces with the textures and tones of the dresser/chest of drawers, bench and Aubusson rug.

OPPOSITE & ABOVE *An abundance of flowering potted plants gives the pergola setting a distinctly French flair. "We use this space all the time," says Angela. "I do my flower arranging and always have my morning coffee out here. It's also a fabulous spot for dinner parties. I especially love it when the grapevine grows wild and covers the entire pergola."*

LEFT *Angela is always playing with containers of various shapes and materials to show off plants and produce. Here, a cast-iron urn filled with digitalis is placed next to a shapely, patinated vasque.*

"My mother had the most amazing garden. The scent of her roses and lilacs still lingers in my memory."

ABOVE *"I have all of my mother's old paintbrushes," says Sandra. She also collects vintage paint palettes, sculptures and landscapes. Some of her favorites hang over her desk in the studio.*

RIGHT *A vintage line drawing by Matisse and a copy of one by Picasso flank a Swedish desk and chair. A collection of vintage art books and a French flag fit well within Sandra's carefully curated decor.*

Perfect
Harmony

Back in 1988, the time came for Sandra and Jeff Linderman to move to a larger home, but it had to be the right house in the right neighborhood. It took months before the couple found what they were looking for in Thousand Oaks, California. "It was in good condition but had to be completely remodeled," Sandra recalls. "It was my perfect canvas."

OPPOSITE *Connected by their color palette, items of varied origins, heights, shapes, sizes and finishes create visual and tactile interest without rivaling each other. "Simple doesn't have to be austere," says Sandra. "Pair elegant with casual, practical with decorative and include meaningful items."*

"I'm very drawn to whites, stones and grays, and from there I added a little robin's egg blue with art, pillows and small furnishings."

LEFT *"With the right elements, even the most muted palette can be pretty and homey," says Sandra.* This design tenet is in evidence in the living room, where hints of color added to neutral shades offer a quiet, understated atmosphere. The furnishings represent a variety of styles, from timeless antiques to more contemporary touches.

ABOVE *In the modern kitchen, vintage items including old signage and French linens add a culinary feel with a European flair. Simple glass-fronted white cabinetry keeps cooking staples and everyday dishes handy.*

PAGE 80 *Redesigning the kitchen was a must to accommodate the family's entertaining needs. A large island now offers ample space for meals. French barstools provide movable seating, while pendant lights add industrial chic.*

JEFF IS A BUILDER and Sandra is a designer and antiques dealer, so they took on the task of updating the 1966-built house as a team. Creating more space was the first priority. "Our vision for our home was an open concept, all white walls and natural wood floors," Sandra explains. "Jeff and I worked together to bring the plan to fruition. He did all the construction and I was in charge of the design."

As a foundation for Sandra's streamlined interiors style, Jeff expanded the master bedroom and garage and made the kitchen and dining room into one large area—perfect for cooking, entertaining and even impromptu dance parties. They share the home with their grown children Jeffrey, Sarah and Emily, and the layout brings everyone together. "We love to have family and friends over, so we focused on simplicity, functionality and natural light," says Sandra.

With the new layout in place, it was time for Sandra to take the lead on the interior decoration. Her trademark palette of pale neutrals and interesting textures abounds in every room, always punctuated with accents in dusty hues that underscore her harmonious aesthetic. "I'm very drawn to whites, stones and grays, and from there I added a little robin's egg blue with art, pillows and small furnishings."

Art has always played a large part in Sandra's life. "My mother was an artist and a big influence in my love for antiques and interior design," she explains. "When something inspired her, she would immediately draw or paint it. Our home was all white and acted as a gallery for her work. She also loved scouring antiques stores looking for hidden treasures." Sandra grew up surrounded by creativity and today that inherited reverence for beauty is evident at every turn.

Like her mother, Sandra has a sense of urgency when she sees something she admires. "After years of treasure hunting, antiques became a passion of mine," she says. "I am inspired by the French countryside and love all things French!" She expertly mixes favorite items—made of old wood, wearing worn paint or showing signs of benign neglect—with Swedish and Americana pieces. Storied possessions such as art, old books, vintage linen, sculptures and horse figures are also added to the mix.

ABOVE *A 3-foot/90cm-tall papier-mâché Champagne bottle—originally used as a store display in France—and a bakery sign create a fitting visual that communicates the connection between the kitchen and the dining area.*

ABOVE *Jeff built the 8-foot/2.4-meter top for the dining-room table to fit over vintage French sawhorses/ trestles. The cabinet, also from France, hosts favorite collections including confit pots and iconic Steiff cats.*

OPPOSITE BELOW LEFT *In the foyer, a Louis-Philippe mirror is paired with a blue chest and a wooden horse. These three items, all from France, reflect the themes and hues found throughout the home.*

RIGHT *"My daughter Emily and I often paint together in the studio," Sandra explains. "It's our sacred space." Character-rich pieces such as the French chaise, bench and oval desk, meaningful artwork and a fresh color scheme sustain Sandra's considered approach to design.*

BELOW RIGHT *Sandra's way of displaying artwork is both relaxed and stylish, as illustrated by the way she uses an easel to prop a painting and a vintage palette. Framed portraits are casually set on the floor below the French sign on the wall.*

"I am inspired by the French countryside and love all things French!"

Sandra loves nothing more than to find old furniture and restore it to its former glory. The only problem is deciding what to keep for herself, what to swap with friends and what to sell through her business as an antiques dealer.

She shares a space with her friend Sydney in two well-curated shops in Southern California, one at The Mart Collective antiques mall in Venice and the other at Summerland Antique Collective in Santa Barbara. "We bring new pieces every week," says Sandra. "It's a great way to part with things in order to keep my home looking fresh and curated."

One foundational French decorating tip is to let the eye travel through a space with clear points of interest, a concept Sandra executes perfectly in every room. For instance, in the living room a bust of Caesar positioned on a sculptor's desk offers an intriguing decorative element, while eye-catching vintage signage connects the large kitchen and dining area and lends a graphic punch.

Because Sandra favors a curated style, she always looks for authentic pieces, "the older the better, not always perfect," she says.

In her home, cherished things that have made the cut are exhibited in a most thoughtful and uncluttered way that sets a peaceful mood and beautifully elevates her rendition of French design.

PAGES 84–85 *As throughout the home, comfort, simplicity and restraint rule the master bedroom. Strokes of Sandra's favored blues from vintage textiles and bedding add texture and allure to whites and grays.*

BELOW *In keeping with her unfussy aesthetic, Sandra selected bathroom elements that combine function with timeless charm. The demilune marble-topped vanity and antique mirror are united by their color, while a chinoiserie jar and garden roses elicit French finesse.*

OPPOSITE *A trumeau mirror reflects a horse figure on an apothecary's chest, which offers ample storage as well as display space. "I love pieces with lots of drawers," Sandra says. A wicker French Champagne basket that was once used for picking grapes keeps extra blankets within reach.*

ABOVE *The bedroom has a seating area that leads to the bathroom. To divide the spaces, Jeff installed a pair of French doors Sandra found at an antiques show. Rather than a traditional towel rack, Sandra chose a blue-painted ladder. A gilded mirror provides balance with the more rustic items.*

2

La Vie est Belle

ABOVE & RIGHT *Fresh flowers are presented in a vintage planter. True to her sense of display, Kathy shows off antique serving domes in an intriguing radial arrangement on either side of the mirrors. The balanced yet asymmetrical placement is in keeping with the couple's relaxed style.*

Cultivated
Charm

OPPOSITE *The front door opens into a small, elegant foyer that foretells the home's soft blue and neutral palette. Arched openings between rooms speak of the charming original architecture. A discreet chandelier offers the first note of French flair.*

When Kathy and Doug McCabe moved from a large home in a gated community in Dallas, Texas to a small cottage in the quaint town of McKinney, both life and style changed. Kathy, an interior designer and shop owner with over 25 years' experience, welcomed the move and the shift. "We were coming out of a more ornate, heavy European trend in design," she says. "So it was the right time to lighten up to a softer look." Though vintage French and European pieces remain the couple's favorites, this time around they chose items fitting a cottage aesthetic. "They just seem right for this house," says Kathy.

THIS PAGE & RIGHT *Though not expansive, the living room manages to accommodate two sofas without feeling weighed down. Similarly, the simple coffee table keeps the design scheme on the lighter side. The muted palette and well-chosen accessories contribute to the cottage's classic French country look.*

THE 2,400-SQUARE-FOOT/223-SQUARE-METER HOME is situated in the historic district of this storied Texas town, a couple of blocks away from Kathy's shop My Favorite Room. It is a setting where she is free to experiment with the pieces she loves to collect—simple items sourced from old farmhouses in the French countryside and similar ones acquired Stateside.

The story-and-a-half vintage cottage hadn't been updated through the years. Though the couple didn't want to alter the scale or the external façade, they agreed that the original floor plan needed some modifications. "The interiors really reflected what was going on in home design back in the day," says Kathy. "It was all about small doors, small walls and small rooms."

To maximize the existing layout, she and Doug opened up the spaces by bumping out bay windows, and by widening every interior doorway the structure allowed. With thoughtful planning and design savvy, they addressed the things that bothered them most. For example, the kitchen, dining room and living room were closed off from one another. "Now we can see all the way from the front door to the back wall," Kathy says. "That kind of openness creates a whole different feeling."

Once walled off from both the kitchen and living room, this sunny space serves as a dining room and library. Now the kitchen can be screened off using antique French doors with leaded glass. These are suspended on barn-door tracks that are hidden by the crown molding/cornice.

Kathy relied on her love of repurposing vintage finds and her longtime partnership with Dallas contractor FERCO Construction to draw on and amplify the home's distinctly cottage character. Now that the kitchen is open to the living areas, the McCabes wanted the option to provide some closure when needed. The answer came in the form of vintage French doors mounted on a barn-door track, which can be pulled closed to conceal work in progress in the kitchen or left open for an airy feel.

To highlight the artisanal, handmade character of the home's furnishings and architecture, Kathy chose a restful palette. Against a subtle backdrop of soft gray and dusty blue, natural wood finishes ground the rooms and enhance the prevalent atmosphere, which is soft, chic and serene.

OPPOSITE BELOW LEFT & THIS PAGE *Clever details—such as the pedestal "legs" on either side of the range/cooker—give built-ins the look of freestanding furniture in a European country kitchen. To make the island,* Kathy repurposed a long sideboard that was once open to the lower shelf. It now has a central section with warming drawers on one side (facing the sink) and faux drawer fronts on the other.

Previously a detached one-car garage, this graceful room is now an extra entertaining space. A built-in buffet keeps necessities at hand, plus its top surface acts as a serving and pass-through area when the bifold windows are open. Slipcovered chairs and a fitted, ruffled tablecloth bring just the right dash of elegance.

Keeping pattern minimal and choosing cotton and linen fabrics add to the French country charm and further cultivate the home's subdued elegance.

In the end, the house reflects Kathy's design touchstone: character. "Character is most important to me," she says. "Even more so than what style a piece represents. I like using things you aren't going to see in a lot of homes to give a house a unique personality. I get much satisfaction turning vintage finds into unique accents to make beautiful objects live once again."

ABOVE *This little sitting room is the perfect spot to enjoy morning coffee or an evening drink. Dressmaker details— from the ottoman's skirted slipcover to the ruffle-trimmed pillows—lend subtle texture. Kathy establishes a serene and uncluttered mood by keeping furnishings to a minimum, but every piece embodies French elegance, simplicity and style.*

ABOVE *In a home with a mostly neutral palette, a room full of pattern is a pleasant surprise. In black and white, this toile de Jouy wallpaper adds cottage character to the attic space without detracting from the home's calming neutrality. Deep dormers offer space for cozy extra seating.*

LEFT *This vaulted upstairs space, reserved for her grandchildren when they come to visit, is one of Kathy's favorite rooms in which to grab some quiet time. "Even when the babies outgrow the crib," she says, "most of the other elements here will stay the same. This room just feels good."*

LEFT *Delicate details spruce up the bathroom, including the damask wallpaper, crystal chandelier and iron chair. The items all add a lacy motif in keeping with the home's French finesse. The soothing combination of the soft blue walls with the white, diaphanous curtains and clawfoot slipper tub confers a spa-like aura.*

BELOW *The French embrace the "hearth and home" lifestyle. To achieve this sought-after look, Kathy mixes wood pieces in a variety of natural finishes with metals that show a little age. In lieu of conventional artwork, a display of porcelain platters creates a soft focal point below a weathered zinc canopy.*

"I get much satisfaction turning vintage finds into unique accents to make beautiful objects live once again."

ABOVE & RIGHT *"My husband Gordon and I had a wonderful time finding these old canvasses at flea markets throughout France," says Renée. Displayed on an antique, weatherworn étagère are items found during the couple's travels or received as gifts from friends.*

OPPOSITE *With its Provençal colors and earthy textures, the kitchen has the charming sunflower yellow hues of a Van Gogh painting. Cushy pillows, cheerful window curtains and a small crystal chandelier soften the heft of the stone table.*

En *Provence*

The address is Southern California, but the home of Renée Parker feels as though it has been airlifted from the French countryside, most specifically Provence. Just say the name and visions appear of endless purple lavender, golden sunflowers, crimson poppy fields and open-air food markets overflowing with fresh breads, cheeses, buckets of olives, braids of garlic and so much more. Anyone who walks through Renée's rooms cannot help feeling a longing for that serene lifestyle, lovingly recreated with mementoes of a lifelong journey.

RENÉE, A FORMER FLIGHT ATTENDANT who flew in the heyday of air travel, thinks of her home as an album come to life, with every object telling a story—one that begins in the 1960s when she graduated from training school, outfitted with a sky blue uniform and pillbox hat.

While based in New Orleans, where she still has a home (featured in this book on pages 170–177), Renée fell in love with the French culture, which is so prevalent in the famous city. "The atmosphere and the parks left me with a lasting impression of how I would like to live."

England, Ireland, Italy, Spain—Renée visited them all, always finding time to tour historic sites and gorgeous gardens. France in particular won her heart, whether she was exploring the famous gardens of the Impressionist painter Claude Monet in Giverny, the estate of Joséphine Bonaparte— at one time the site of Europe's largest rose collection—or visiting Île de Ré, an island off the west coast of France famous for its the profusions of hollyhocks.

A particularly fateful twist happened when Renée was selected to make Switzerland her temporary home base. "I knew then after that experience that I could live in Europe." Renée continued to touch down around the globe, often having layovers in California, another favorite destination.

After she met her late husband Gordon Werner through a mutual friend, life took another turn. Gordon's profession as a merchant banker took him to Europe for a few years.

PAGES 102 & 103 *In rehabilitating the old stable, Renée and Gordon took care to retain its original features and respect its roots— literally! Witness the trunk of an old trumpet vine growing out of the kitchen floor. The green marble-topped island was once used in a French grocery shop. An enamel towel rack spells out appropriate functions.*

LEFT *The frescoed living-room wall panels once belonged to a French château. The couple incorporated them as a reminder of the many beautiful* maisons de maître *and estates that they toured and stayed in over the years. A pair of* bergères, *marble-topped tables and a vintage rug are highly à propos.*

OPPOSITE ABOVE & BELOW *The salon-style living room features many shelves for treasured volumes. Together with a prized grand piano, the books bring warmth and charm to the sophisticated space. Green shutters temper the elegance of the room. A toile screen conceals an intimate seating nook with a settee plumped with pillows from many countries, including one with a red bird motif that was purchased from a French household.*

"We were dating at that time, and he asked me where in Europe he should live so that I would visit him," says Renée. "Without a doubt I picked Paris! Over time, Gordon was amazed how fond he, too, became of everything French."

Eventually, the couple decided to make their home in Santa Barbara, where Gordon owned a derelict 1912 stable. Here, Renée could indulge her love of gardens. "The property became my passion," she says. "The lifestyle in Santa Barbara lends itself to what we had experienced in the countryside of France." The climate was another consideration. "We concluded that the Parisian winters were so harsh that we would be happier in California and could create 'everything French' right here."

The transformation began with bringing in stone and ironwork, and even walls from a French château. Though the whole building was reconfigured and upgraded, the work was done with respect for elements that could be salvaged to retain the structure's original rustic character.

ABOVE *Unlike the vibrancy of the kitchen or the sophistication of the living room, the main bedroom assumes a low-key, earthy composure. It has a subdued palette, woven furnishings, tactile fabrics and meaningful accents that promote a sense of ease, relaxation and harmony. The maps and globe nod to the couple's travels.*

These included an impressive 100-year-old trumpet vine, which had taken root in what would become the kitchen. Everywhere, French flair has been infused with style and sentiment.

Renée's no-fuss approach to decor imbues each space with a warm and inviting aesthetic and genuine old-world heart. Throughout the house, formal and informal collide in the most wonderful and unexpected ways. For instance, while the living room's frescoed walls, crystal chandelier, period mirror and subdued palette denote a classic sophistication, the kitchen tells a different story. Its textural finishes, vibrant colors and distinctive fabrics express the soul of rural France.

OPPOSITE *Renée lets her inner romantic take charge in the library, where a soft palette is enriched by the warmth of luxurious velvet and silk fabrics and an abundance of rare leather-bound tomes. Artwork also contributes to the room's intimate atmosphere. Set in this private refuge, a French daybed invites all to peruse favorite books or simply dream in quiet comfort.*

That same spirit extends to Renée's beloved garden, where antique statuary and stonework cohabit with humble rusty buckets and verdigris urns in typical French abandon. Pathways and private seating tucked here and there create the mood of an old country inn.

The once dilapidated stables and neglected grounds have been affectionately reimagined as a stylish enclave with all the charming appeal of a Provençal farmhouse and flourishing gardens that reconnect the home to its surroundings. Here is where Renée's day begins with morning coffee on the terrace—together with her rescued pup, aptly named "Merci Beaucoup." Lunch is served on the raised deck overlooking the ocean with a glass of wine or a pastis, a popular aperitif in the South of France. The essence of *joie de vivre*!

THIS PAGE & OPPOSITE *A passionate gardener, Renée built this garden room adjacent to the kitchen. In keeping with the authenticity of the French homes she had visited, she incorporated salvaged windows, brick flooring and cement walls and banquettes that she finished with an aged patina. Black-and-white toile cushions soften the seating spots, while statuary, urns and metal containers bring more garden goods in. This is where Renée starts seeds, prepares lavish homegrown bouquets and studies botanical books.*

OPPOSITE The magnificent, rescued trumpet vine now drapes along the whole length of the front of the home. A bicycle recalls scenes from a French village market, with a basket filled with flowers. Lavender and fragrant herbs make the terrace a favorite spot for alfresco meals.

LEFT Little sheltered nooks pepper the grounds. Here, Renée added an awning, a crystal chandelier and a vintage mirror to perpetuate the French look she adores. California's balmy climate allows many flower varieties to thrive, among them hydrangeas and agapanthus.

BELOW LEFT Pastis, a popular French aperitif, is traditionally enjoyed before dinner. However, on weekends it's often sipped throughout the day while playing pétanque.

BELOW The free-flowing garden has evolved over time. Renée grows all the herbs that that she cooks with, including wild arugula/rocket, French tarragon and, of course, lavender, to name a few. A classic garden urn planted with strawberries creates the look of a potager.

"The property became my passion. The lifestyle in Santa Barbara lends itself to what we had experienced in the countryside of France."

OPPOSITE *Soft blues, country reds and ocher yellows are the basis for the kitchen's decor. The upper cabinets match the room's trim, while the lower ones sport a rich crimson hue. In true farmhouse fashion, a fabric skirt covers the plumbing below an aged copper sink.*

ABOVE *The upper portion of this trumeau mirror, with its painted scene of children playing with a dog, proved irresistible for Penelope. It now resides in the main hall.*

RIGHT *In an antique Welsh hutch/dresser, open shelves showcase a variety of colorful hand-painted plates and mugs, including Penelope's extensive collection of vintage Happy Bird china.*

Continental *Élan*

When interior designer Penelope Bianchi and her husband Adam discovered a lovely parcel of land wedged between a nature reserve and a historic estate in Montecito, they snapped it up and created an oasis where Southern California meets the South of France. "We'd been looking to buy a house, not build one," says Penelope. But when they fell in love with the 2.5-acre/1-hectare lot, the couple soon changed their minds.

Two antique valances/pelmets were sewn together to create the one that runs the length of the window seat. Chic pillows add to the celebration of textile artistry. The French armchairs were inherited from Adam's uncle. The wicker trunk holds a miniature indoor orchid garden.

PENELOPE AND ADAM HAVE BUILT A ONE-STORY, stucco-covered home, a guest cottage and a separate garage, all clustered around a courtyard in a way that evokes a traditional French farm. "The land around the house reminded me of Provence," Penelope recalls. "So we traveled there and photographed many things that inspired us: doors, shutters, roofs and more."

The quaint appearance of the home's walls, both inside and out, was achieved by tinting plaster with natural pigments mined out of the ground in Roussillon, a village in the Luberon area that is famous for its pink ocher. On their return from Provence, the Bianchis brought back the precious pigment in a multitude of small bags.

Designed to be a subtle backdrop for Penelope's eclectic collection of antique furniture and fabrics, the limewashed interior walls also possess a gentle patina. "By adding slightly different amounts of pigment, we were able to somewhat vary the color of each space," she explains.

ABOVE *Pigments from Roussillon have been mixed with lime, then applied onto raw plaster to create a mellow hue for the walls. The front door was custom-made by a local artist, while the Chinese plates came from Penelope's grandmother and the carved pieces from Adam's uncle's collection.*

Inside the 4,000-square-foot/372-square-meter home, the rooms unfold in an engaging tapestry of patterns and colors with a blend of pieces from various origins. "To me, a house should be an autobiography or a scrapbook of who lives there," says Penelope. "From the pieces we have collected over the years and those passed on from Adam's family and mine, everything in our home has a story."

Inspired by the design of an ancient farmhouse, there is a 33-foot/10-meter-long "big hall" with a living room at one end, a dining room at the other and a cozy informal sitting area in the middle. Identical fireplaces anchor each end of the space, topped with trumeau mirrors found in a shop in New Orleans. "Above one of the mirrors was a painted scene of children playing with a dog that looked like ours, so I had to have them," Penelope recalls. "It's one of my favorite rooms. It is filled with things I love." That includes an infusion of chinoiserie that she enjoys for their whimsical and evocative motifs.

Many of the Bianchis' found treasures and family heirlooms were originally showcased in their previous home. To fill in the additional space their new farmhouse provided, the couple traveled far and wide searching for just the right pieces. After returning from one such excursion with a bounty of items, Adam said, "All we need now are some chickens!"

ABOVE *At one end of the space known as the "great hall," the living room welcomes with a cozy fireplace and furniture dressed in blue floral slipcovers that Penelope uses during the summer. In winter, she switches them for a set featuring red hues and cheerful stripes.*

OPPOSITE *During the Renaissance, the rooster became a symbol of the French nation. It's fitting that Penelope would display the ceramic rooster and chicken gifted by her neighbor on the dining-room table. Chinese art and furnishings mingle with inherited family pieces.*

"To me, a house should be an autobiography or a scrapbook of who lives there."

"Adam's grandfather immigrated from Italy to California as a boy," Penelope explains. "Years later, he established the first commercial poultry business on the West Coast." So, they had a coop built and soon had their own flock of Mille Fleur bantam hens. "When they are clucking cheerfully it can get noisy," Penelope admits. "A few years after we moved in, Oprah Winfrey bought the property next door. One day, I came home and found a phone message from our new neighbor."

The message explained that a journalist had reported that Oprah did not like living next door to the Bianchis' chickens. "It is absolutely not true," said Oprah on the recording. As a kind gesture, a beautifully wrapped box arrived by mail with a gorgeous ceramic rooster and hen inside. The card, signed by Oprah, read, "Contrary to tabloid opinion, I love your chickens!"

OPPOSITE *In the middle of the great hall, chairs and ottomans stand ready to be moved around to fit any gatherings. Easily accessible, the table is used for seasonal displays or as a bar and food station for cocktail parties. The handmade tiles are from Mexico, but their shape and color are in keeping with those found in old European homes.*

LEFT *The master bathroom's focal point is a handsome 19th-century zinc-lined copper tub that was made in Paris in the 1860s.*

Penelope brought in the recurring Chinese motif by hanging a birdcage with a pagoda-like design overhead. Throughout the home, windows are painted in a custom French blue-gray.

ABOVE *Colors and patterns come together to give the main bedroom its inviting appeal. A pillow made from a silk-screen print by French artist Marcel Vertès is given pride of place on the bed. The antique armoire holds a large collection of decorating books. A vintage dhurrie warms the terracotta tiles.*

One of the things that attracted Penelope to this property was the surrounding nature. "I've always loved animals and all the land was a big draw," she says. "In fact, the thing I love most about our home is where it is." The couple's rescue dogs, Peugeot the French Poodle and Pete the Corgi mix, both agree. Penelope continues: "Adam and I are constantly amazed by our good fortune at finding a quiet corner of California where we could create a little bit of paradise."

OPPOSITE *The loggia is Penelope's favorite outdoor spot. A French limestone table and benches, with a combined weight of several tons, are impervious to wind and rain. It took 10 men to lift them into place.*

ABOVE *Right off the kitchen and surrounded by fragrant herbs, flowers and majestic trees, a beautifully weathered table and*

chairs and an iron chandelier offer a dreamy setting for casual or elaborate garden parties.

RIGHT *Evocative of homes in the Provençal countryside, stone steps and statuary lead the way to the front door, painted the same shade of blue as the windows. Lush ivy and fragrant climbing roses drape across the pink plaster façade.*

3

Heritage Style

ABOVE & RIGHT *"The large chalkboard was already in its ornate frame when I bought it at the Long Beach Antique Market," says Laurence. "I liked the idea that I could leave messages for my children and my husband before leaving the house."*

Belle
Brocante

OPPOSITE *While on a trip home to France, Laurence purchased these Louis XV medallion chairs from an antiques dealer in Lyon. The farm table was a local flea-market score and the shutters, frame and sconce hail from a brocante in Montréal, where the family used to live.*

Both Laurence and Christophe Gomez were born in France, and when you enter their California home, their heritage is evident. "My father was an interior decorator," Laurence explains. "He loved antiques, and I inherited his passion. Since I was little, I loved to visit my dad in his antiques shop or in his workshop. Whenever we were out for a drive and he saw a roadside sign announcing 'Antiques' ahead, he just had to stop. It was impossible for him to miss a treasure! I do the same. It's in my DNA."

CHRISTOPHE'S WORK AS AN EXECUTIVE producer for video games dictated the couple's numerous moves, beginning in 1996 when they relocated to London. "Then other destinations followed," Laurence says. "San Francisco, Los Angeles, Montréal and then back to Los Angeles." Although they have lived in various homes through the years, one thing remained constant: their love of France and its antiques. "All my family is in Burgundy," says Laurence. "We go home for a vacation at least once a year, sometimes more." And during each of her trips, Laurence visits the many brocantes of the region. "I miss them so much," she says. "Here, the next best thing are weekend flea markets, which I attend regularly."

When the couple moved back to Los Angeles from Montréal in 2011, they almost passed on their current 1942 cottage in Tarzana. At 1,900 square feet/176 square meters, it was much smaller than any of their previous homes, but it had a lot of charm. "And the location was perfect because it was close to schools for our sons Maxence and Samuel, and to Christophe's office," Laurence explains. Another plus was the front porch: "I fell in love with it," she says. And though the home needed major cosmetic improvements, no structural ones were required.

"The interior was dark—the walls were yellow and brown, furniture blocked the windows and the old carpet had to go," Laurence recalls. "I immediately reimagined it with white everywhere, wooden floors and lots of natural light coming in." Her aim was to create a *"douce ambience,"* a soothing atmosphere. "Above all, I wanted a cozy house. I like having little nooks like the breakfast area and other places to relax."

To that end, she relied on paint colors such as Cool December from Behr and Benjamin Moore's White Wisp for the walls. Nantucket Gray, also from Benjamin Moore, can be seen on the window frames. Once the new wood flooring was in place, it was time to give way to her passion: decorating with the vintage pieces she loves and bringing her French roots into focus.

"I am so connected to the beautiful materials, fabrics, antiques and everything from the past," says Laurence. "They have so much charm and history." In fact, when the couple's now grown sons left home to live on their own, Maxence in Paris and Samuel in Los Angeles, it is that appreciation and knowledge that compelled Laurence to open her successful online shop French Broc, where she offers items and objects gleaned from her trips back home.

"I am so connected to the beautiful materials, fabrics, antiques and everything from the past."

PAGES 126 & 127 *A French sign offers a warm welcome. The cozy breakfast room is one of Laurence's favorite spaces. "It holds many meaningful items, such as the table from Lyon and the chairs from Paris," she says. "I also collect old domes and silverware, particularly monogrammed cutlery. Antique household linens are another passion of mine."*

LEFT *From the vintage daybed and pillows to the patinated coffee table, many of the items in this room remind Laurence of her youth, especially the shutters. "For me they are the memory of my childhood in Nice—they are the true symbol of the city."*

Meaningful pieces from Laurence's family are also an intrinsic part of her interior. "It's a way to be close to them," she says. One particular item exemplifies that connection. "My dad once gave me a *fauteuil de maîtrise*, or master's armchair. It's a small piece of furniture created for a training program by candidates who wanted to become masters after six years of apprenticeship in the 18th century. I love the story and that it's a gift from my dad."

That unique piece alone eloquently speaks of Laurence's familial ties and her reverence for her French heritage. A livable space with character is the essence of traditional French interior design, with comfort and personality at its heart.

"The sofa and armchair are the only new pieces in the living room," says Laurence, who has a fondness for old clockfaces. "There are objects that attract us, and for me it's antique timepieces. I just can't resist when I find one." Old linen grain sacks repurposed as textiles underscore the quintessential French aesthetic.

RIGHT *Even as a child, Laurence was fond of elegant dishware. "I always loved ironstone. It reminds me of my grandmothers' beautiful homes and the pretty tables they would set."*

BELOW *When the couple bought the cottage, the existing kitchen got a facelift with white paint and the island was reborn in a soft gray hue. Laurence proudly displays her grandmother's set of scales: "It holds a lot of sentimental value."*

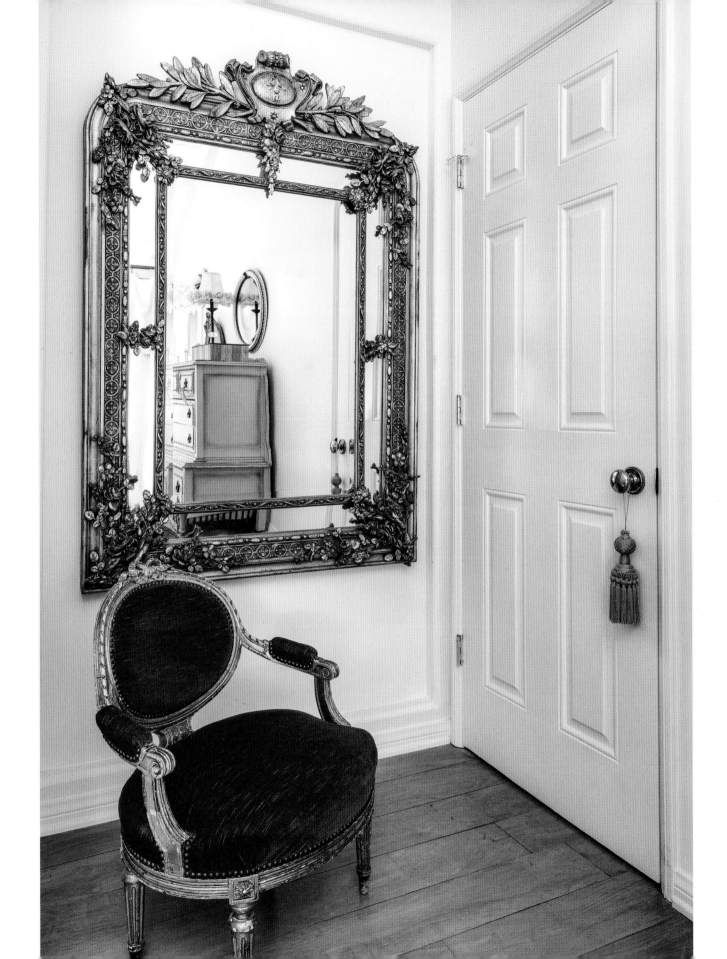

OPPOSITE *An ornately gilded flea-market mirror and a priceless* fauteuil de maître *(master's armchair) in its original upholstery, sent over from France by Laurence's father, set a regal tone in a corner of the bedroom.*

ABOVE *"This setting reminds me a little of my years as a ballet dancer, especially the old prom dress," Laurence recalls. "And the white chair belonged to my grandmother—France and family are all around me!"*

RIGHT *Though partial to white, Laurence likes to inject some color accents here and there. An original 1900s French Provincial dresser/chest of drawers featuring hand-painted details makes an elegant and feminine statement while adding a nuanced hue to the pristine space.*

ABOVE *"The garden table has been with me since my childhood in Nice. I won't part with it,"* Laurence says. *"The vintage enamel street sign is from another favorite collection of mine."*

LEFT *Grown in hedges, single plants or in pots, rosemary is a staple of Mediterranean gardens and a major component of French cooking. Laurence keeps some on hand to add to recipes as well as for its fragrant and decorative appeal.*

RIGHT *Californian weather offers conditions similar to the South of France. Taking full advantage of this, Laurence and Christophe have planted aromatic herbs, sweet lavender and perfumed roses in their garden, not only for their beauty but also for their benefits to pollinators.*

Je pense qu'il y un petit enfant
dans tous d'entre nous et nous
tous pour souvent
oublier de lib·erer
l'enfant pour jouer

OPPOSITE & ABOVE *Found in a vintage shop, a harvest table and wood and wicker chairs offer a rustic counterpoint to a crystal chandelier. The French poster captured Chantal's heart the moment she saw it. Branches of lemons are displayed in a pitcher.*

RIGHT *An antique baker's rack speaks of the durability of humble, well-made pieces. On its shelves, dishware with a nature-inspired pattern has become part of the dining room's French farmhouse aesthetic. A small cabinet and a still-life painting complete the evocative, down-to-earth decor.*

French
Kissed

There are some things that never cease to tug at the heart of Chantal Cloutier: love of nature, animals, homes, simple French interiors and a pure palette. Bringing together all these elements, her home in Solvang, California represents a return to her roots.

"MY MOTHER WAS FRENCH-CANADIAN and she married an American," Chantal recalls. "I was the only one of our large family born in California, but as a young child, I returned to live in the quiet countryside outside Montréal with my aunts, uncles and cousins." It was a formative experience. "Our family always had a strong connection to nature. We were brought up with the four seasons and the outdoors was our playground."

It was the love of her family and their simple, seasonal lifestyle that, when she was in her thirties, compelled her to buy a cabin of her own in Québec. It nestles on 80 acres/32.4 hectares in the Laurentians, one of the oldest mountain regions in the world. "I still own the cabin and it remains my favorite home," she says, adding, "And it was the first time I discover flea-market shopping as a way to furnish and decorate an interior."

After Chantal's parents divorced, she and her mother moved to Los Angeles where Chantal began a career in modeling. "One day, I was walking home from school— I must have been 5 feet 10 inches and about 11 years old,"

she recalls. "A lady with a French accent asked if I would model for one of her paintings. I remember that painting being 6 feet tall. That's how my modeling career began and it continued until I was in my thirties." At that point, she decided to start her own modeling agency. "I was fortunate to have interned for many years under the wing of Franklin Welsh and Paul Jasmin, two talented men in the beauty and fashion arenas. It was the right time, the right place and the right people helping each other."

Chantal understands the positive results that come with kindness and thoughtfulness. Case in point, a letter she received years ago from a stranger named Michael Blake, asking if he could rent her former home in Topanga Canyon. "He had no credit and no money, but he told me he had just finished writing a book and would soon have the necessary funds. I trusted him," she recalls. As fate would have it, shortly thereafter, Michael was nominated and won an Academy Award for his screen adaptation of that same book: *Dances With Wolves*.

ABOVE *A small side table makes just the right perch for a fragrant candle and a ceramic flowerpot.*
OPPOSITE *A street sign and enamel wall bins were discovered at a traveling antique show.*

ABOVE *The original farmhouse cabinet has moved with Chantal from one home to the next. "I found it in a now-defunct vintage shop many years ago," she recalls. A birdcage-style chandelier presides over a floor pillow with authentic embroidery, acquired at a friend's moving sale.*

OPPOSITE *A Louis XVI hall tree is the star of the entryway. With hooks, a mirror, a console and umbrella stands, it performs multiple functions with grace and elegance. Over time, the hand-painted finish has acquired a lovely patina.*

Chantal had long been an animal advocate, rescuing countless senior dogs, but of her connection with Michael, she says "He opened my eyes to the plight of old horses." That week, she brought home seven horses that were destined for a slaughterhouse. That was 25 years ago, but of the years she spent saving animals Chantal says, "It remains my life's most essential and rewarding time." Today, she shares her home with True Ami, a 10-year-old rescue Labrador.

Chantal says she always knew her roots were in France. "I learned early on that my ancestors immigrated from La Rochelle to Gravelbourg, a small multicultural town in Canada." She loves all things French and has visited the country numerous times. "I always start in Paris, then venture off to discover as much of the country as possible by car, bike or barge."

"I always value authenticity and quality over quantity."

Upon moving into the loft, Chantal painted all the rooms white, including the bricks of the original fireplace. White slipcovered furnishings maintain the purity of the palette. The two large mirrors are some of the few she kept when she downsized from her previous home. An elegant table and a rustic bench offset each other while keeping the color scheme intact.

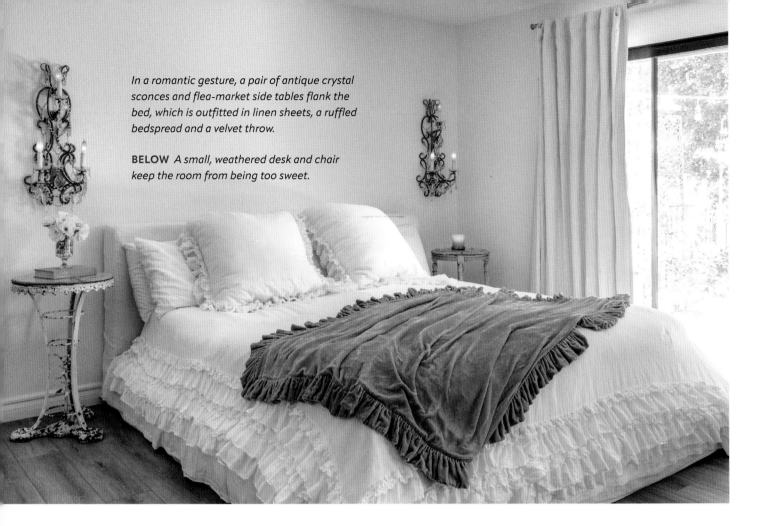

In a romantic gesture, a pair of antique crystal sconces and flea-market side tables flank the bed, which is outfitted in linen sheets, a ruffled bedspread and a velvet throw.

BELOW *A small, weathered desk and chair keep the room from being too sweet.*

She has managed to incorporate her preferred interior style in her present abode in Solvang. "I specifically visualized a place that had a loft-style feel," she says. "What I love about many French interiors is that they are clean and uncluttered, and they don't follow decorating rules." That uncontrived design ethos is evident in her sparsely yet cozily furnished rooms. She transformed the previously gloomy, dreary space into a light-filled sanctuary.

To impart character to the loft, Chantal turned to vintage pieces that she has owned for 30 years or more—from mirrors to farm-style cabinets. "I always value authenticity and quality over quantity," she notes. That mantra comes fully into focus with rustic yet refined antiques. Their off-the-shoulder elegance lends a French minimalist appeal and highlights the beauty found in the humble and imperfect.

And let's not forget that the French have an unwavering love for their pets. So, it's no surprise that Chantal would conclude, "A home without an animal is not a home."

Chantal chose a pedestal sink, similar to those found in small Parisian hotels, for the serene bathroom. The Louis XVI-style nightstand has found a new purpose here, offering both charm and function. Its gently weathered, textural finish evokes an artisanal touch, which is accentuated by an original glass cabinet.

OPPOSITE *To give the petite kitchen a welcoming atmosphere, the couple painted the walls a soft dusty pink, Setting Plaster by Farrow & Ball. Rather than add more built-in cabinetry, they incorporated furniture they already owned to create an unfitted arrangement inspired by traditional European kitchens.*

ABOVE & RIGHT *The Gallic rooster, France's national bird, makes a fitting emblem for Sue's kitchen decor. Assorted French copper pots and pans, a vintage American kettle, Polish pottery inherited from her mother and an Italian stove/cooker impart an international flavor. Hand-scraped bamboo flooring contributes organic texture underfoot.*

Country *Comfort*

Sue and Tim Johnson's charming petite maison in Phoenix, Arizona, would fit nicely in any of the villages dotted around France. The couple got engaged while visiting Paris and successive trips to France soon followed. "We both fell in love with the smaller homes, brocantes and gardens," says Sue. When you add the fact that half of her father's ancestry is French and that her early school years were spent under the tutelage of French nuns, it's no surprise this confluence of events would influence her aesthetic.

THOUGH THE VINTAGE COTTAGE WITH ITS footprint of 1,100 square feet/102 square meters was smaller than their previous home and in great need of improvements, it offered Sue a blank slate. Its location at the base of a mountain preserve with many hiking trails nearby also played a big part in the couple's decision to buy it. "I liked the big wooden windows and the fact that I could do anything I wanted without restrictions," Sue explains. "Plus, it's at the edge of the city and there are still farms in our neighborhood."

The Johnsons renovated the entire house and added French doors leading from the eating area to an enclosed porch, which provides additional living space as well as a laundry room. They retained the kitchen's original footprint, which suited their need for self-contained spaces. "It was important that the rooms remain separate," says Sue. "Tim works from home and my daughter, who is now a professional pianist, would practice several hours a day."

Over the years those needs changed, and although it remained the same size, the kitchen has evolved. Two years ago it underwent a second remodel. As before, the couple did all the work themselves. "We took it to the next level of a cottage kitchen. I swapped my Swedish stove for one with a French look, painted all the cabinets and changed the lighting," Sue recalls. Meanwhile, Tim built the shelving, modified the cabinets to accommodate the new stove and created and installed all the moldings and wood panels. He learned his carpentry skills from his father and grandfather, who were both in the trade. "It is my favorite room because we both put our hearts, souls and hands into it," says Sue.

The same mood extends to the rest of the home, where furniture with classic shapes and a little patina is complemented by relaxed fabrics: plain linens and some prints, stripes and checks. "I gravitate to furniture based on Louis XV and Louis XVI styles because the designs are elegant without being pretentious, but I also like wicker and some rustic wood," Sue notes. "I must love something to buy it and it must fit the scale of the space. However, I have one tall piece in each room because it creates the illusion of the spaces being bigger than they actually are."

ABOVE & OPPOSITE *Iconic dishes designed by French chef Jacques Pépin are perfectly at home in the cozy and charmingly furnished dining space, which invites with its intimate comfort and country appeal.*

Sue is not afraid of colors and prefers muted tones over pastels. Shades of blue, pink, yellow, cream, green and even black are repeated throughout all the rooms of the cottage. "Sometimes, depending on the space, I make one color more dominant than the others," she explains, "but there is always a touch of French blue in every room." The charm of Sue's home comes from the sum of all its parts, from furnishings, colors and authentic elements and materials.

OPPOSITE ABOVE *An antique trumeau mirror adds dimension to the narrow hallway. A pair of topiaries provides symmetry and, along with a dried flower wreath, brings in a touch of nature. Sue collects original artworks—included here is a favorite landscape by her friend, artist John Enright.*

A rustic cabinet offsets the formality of the family's concert piano. An antique candelabra, a santos figure and a garden bouquet confer a romantic aura on the setting. After experimenting with several rugs, Sue opted for a vintage one. Feminine and floral upholstery gives vintage Ethan Allen armchairs a nostalgic allure.

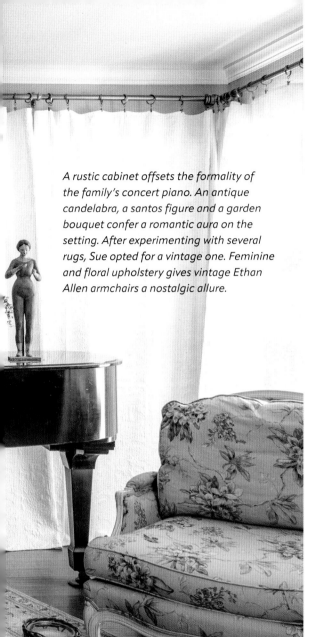

RIGHT *Farrow & Ball's Oval Room Blue imparts a luminescent glow to the library. The vintage chairs appealed to Sue because of their tweed-like upholstery. The painted clock has a theatrical presence. Tim added moldings to the bookcase and painted it to match the walls for a built-in look.*

These include French copper, Polish and Italian pottery, vintage dishes and paintings. "It's the imperfection of it," she explains. "I wanted to evoke a country atmosphere with a garden, fruit trees and chickens. A home connected to the past and the present and the inside to the outsides. I think we have accomplished that." Indeed, they have.

OPPOSITE *To lighten up the family room's original dark paintwork, Sue painted it with Annie Sloan's Paris Grey and distressed the finish. A rug with a Portuguese tile motif softens the painted cement floor. The wing chair was her first grown-up purchase.*

LEFT *A wrought-iron bed is dressed in white linens from Portugal and an embroidered vintage Ralph Lauren bedcover. Draped lace panels add a luxurious cocooning appeal. A colorful, textured vintage Persian rug brings the ethereal setting down to earth.*

ABOVE *Tim built the fireplace to look as though it was original to the home. A framed chalkboard displays some of Sue's own drawings according to the mood of the moment. Yellow-and-white curtains add country charm.*

OPPOSITE *In Sue's daughter's former bedroom, black walls offer a dramatic backdrop for a vintage Gustavian bed and an antique nightstand. A map of Paris and a bust of Michelangelo's David lend continental flair. A blossoming tree conveys a whimsical mood.*

LEFT *The couple added wood paneling to the lower part of the bathroom walls to reflect the age of the house, which was built more than 80 years ago. A gilded antique mirror hangs over a new vanity, which Sue fell in love with for its shapely marble top.*

ABOVE LEFT *A path bordered by native plants leads to a cozy little backyard hideaway where Sue, like a true French country girl, raises chickens and grows flowers, vegetables and fruit. "The garden is my sanctuary," she says.*

ABOVE *"The garden bedroom was a father-daughter project," Sue explains. "My daughter picked out what she wanted and did the math and measurements with her dad. In her teenage years, this was her room from October to May— because of the climate here, we rarely need heat in the winter."*

4

Storied Past

ABOVE & OPPOSITE *Nature and vintage star together in the Zurians' dining room. Framed by vintage shutters, a farmhouse cabinet on an old workbench hosts collections of ironstone dishes, pitchers and transferware ready for use. "Here or abroad, everywhere I go, I am always looking for them," Kathee notes.*

RIGHT *In the foyer, a circa-1500s trunk with original hardware makes a rugged perch for zinc objects, including a rare dolly tub. A bolt holder from a European fabric factory houses dried branches.*

Authentic
Allure

After raising a family and owning a business in their native California, high-school sweethearts Charley and Kathee Zurian were feeling ready to think about retirement. Those plans changed when Charley was offered the job of research and development engineering manager for an aerospace company in North Carolina, and the couple decided to head east.

"I HAD NEVER LIVED IN COLD WEATHER BEFORE,"
says Kathee, who initially stayed behind and directed
her husband to investigate houses she had spotted online.
"My parents were interior designers, so growing up I was
surrounded by all of the upcoming and current trends,"
she explains. "My favorite pieces were always antiques, and
at 15, I made my first purchase, a humpback trunk that I
still have today." Several years later, she quit her regular job
and immersed herself in her passion. "Once I found French
pieces, I was hooked!" she exclaimed. And so began her
extensive collection of French cabinets, tables, linens, quilts,
enamelware and baskets, many of which she still has today.

A traditional Southern-style brick home in Kernersville
fittted the bill, and then some, at triple the size of their
former house. "I loved the large spaces, high ceilings and
hardwood floors, and the views that span every room and
fill them with light," Kathee says. Taken with the 12-acre/
4.85-hectare homestead and large barn, the Zurians
decided to forgo the notion of downsizing altogether.

ABOVE *Kathee's collection of antique French enamelware has been
more than 40 years in the making. The pieces are highly sought
after for their pretty pastel finishes and delicate floral motifs.*

The vast dining room could easily feel cavernous, but instead it has an intimate vibe thanks to large-scale pieces and natural elements. The narrow 10-foot/3-meter farm table is surrounded by chairs left in their original condition. The French iron bakery rack was Kathee's first find after moving to North Carolina.

Once a sunroom, this space was closed off from the rest of the house with French doors. Kathee and Charley removed them to create the wide-open area that is now the living room. Tall accents such as the orchard ladder keep soaring walls in check without stifling the flow.

ABOVE *For Kathee, collections are more than pretty things to be put on display—they are meant to be used. Whether draped on tables, hung in the kitchen or piled on an old wooden shoe rack, French linens are among her favorite items.*

OPPOSITE *With similar worn brown finishes, a wall-mounted cabinet and a modest table are cleverly paired to create a hutch/dresser for a colorful display of tall pitchers, a covered soup tureen and pots and bowls too pretty to keep behind solid doors.*

By removing the doors that once closed off the former sunroom, Kathee realized her open-plan vision while creating a visual connection that flows from room to room. The neutral walls, bare floors and unadorned windows add to the feeling of quiet simplicity.

ABOVE *Outdoor elements are often incorporated into French-style interiors. A garden statue of a lamb and a bucket of dried hydrangeas set a pastoral scene.*

Kathee has her own antiques business, The French Farmer's Wife, and the barn would accommodate all the pieces she imports from Europe for her customers, as well as those she keeps for herself. The land was very attractive to the couple, too. It has given Charley the opportunity to indulge his love of organic gardening as well as providing plenty of room to roam for Rhyley, Rosie and Piper, the family's three Miniature Australian Shepherds. Another benefit that the North Carolina location offered was the ability for the couple to have live chats with all three of their grown children across time zones: daughter Khrystyn in Germany and sons Dustin and Derek in California.

Upon taking up residence, Kathee removed the home's existing trappings. Out went the ceiling fans, curtains and shades/blinds and in came French chandeliers, architectural salvage and years of collected antiques. Authenticity is a key principle for Kathee's style, and you won't find reproductions anywhere. Instead of on-trend accessories, there are sizable pieces of architectural salvage, such as doors and multipaned windows propped against walls, open cabinets storing in-use antiques and rugged finishes such as weathered iron and chalky zinc. Natural elements, including long branches that stretch from floor to ceiling, soften hard lines and dried wreaths continue the organic feel while introducing a new shape.

Inspired by her adopted surroundings, Kathee has kept the windows mostly bare, with walls painted a creamy linen shade that doesn't compete with the view. Tables and chairs with slender legs allow hardwood flooring to play a starring role. A characteristic French palette is used effectively to introduce both color and pattern: there are carved green columns, a blue cabinet and enamelware with botanical motifs.

Kathee strives to create beautiful spaces that are above all casual. "I am partial to rustic French farmhouse style for its simple, sturdy pieces and the history they hold," she says. "Nothing can be damaged here. Everything is pet and family friendly." The result is a home that extends a cordial invitation to come as you are.

ABOVE & LEFT *Propped-up architectural salvage, a zinc headboard and a primitive bench infuse the master bedroom with weathered allure. A sparkling chandelier and an antique kilim rug bring touches of luxe. In an open cabinet, quilts and linens become part of the decor.*

OPPOSITE *A bed outfitted with ticking, toile de Jouy and burlap imparts a French countryside sensibility to the guest bedroom. The antique shoe rack keeps quilts and extra blankets at the ready. The antique humpback trunk was picked out by Kathee when she was 15.*

OPPOSITE *When visitors drop by, they often head straight to the cheerful galley kitchen. The vibrant mix of colors and textural elements like bricks, shutters, finishes and materials more than compensates for the small size of the room. Doors open onto a secret garden.*

ABOVE *Renée tacked an antique canvas tapestry directly to the wall for a casual look. "Sometimes frames feel fussy," she says.*

RIGHT *In the breakfast nook, an informal garden table and chairs have been elevated with lively French fabric and vintage tableware. In lieu of curtains, flea-market shutters continue the rustic theme.*

Historic
Heirloom

When Renée Parker first set eyes on this Greek Revival building in New Orleans, it was nothing but a façade with evidence of the building's footprint and an overgrown lot. A devastating fire had left the house as a mere shell. Undeterred by the work ahead of her, Renée was determined to bring what was left of the historic home back to its former glory.

AT THE TIME, Renée was a flight attendant with Delta Airlines, which has historical ties to Louisiana. She was looking for a pied-à-terre and fell in love with New Orleans for its energy and charm. "It's one of America's most treasured and historic cities," she says. "The architecture, the music, the food and the gardens, but most of all the people who live there give it its worldly charm."

The house is well situated in the Lower Garden District, a mere 20-minute walk to the French Quarter on charming streets punctuated with squares. The neighborhood is a treasure trove of beautiful homes in styles that were popular from the 1840s through the 1960s. However, this was over 30 years ago when the area was not the desirable enclave it is today. "People thought I was crazy for buying this home," Renée recalls with a laugh.

Greek Revival is often called America's first national style, with examples in all areas of the country that were settled by Europeans before the Civil War. Preserving the original 1840 floor plan was important to Renée, so she saved the old chimneys, measured out the rooms and got to work rebuilding. She even researched what the house would have looked like when it was first built, with verandas out front.

Once the basic structure was in place, Renée set to work on the interiors. Her aim was to create rooms with elements that honored the past while reflecting the dynamism and cultural influences of The Big Easy. With that goal in mind, she filled the house with treasures gathered on her international travels, as well as distinctively local finds. Renée has an uncanny sense for identifying the inherent beauty of pieces others would overlook, like the living-room pier mirror, a New Orleans original she bought at an estate sale on the grand St. Charles Avenue, or the bathroom's Turkish marble sink.

While furnishing the spaces, her focus and vision remained constant. "I'd come up with ideas for using old iron pieces or shutters, and my dear friend Larry Rousell would turn those plans into reality," she recalls. "He made the iron bed and table in my bedroom by welding them, and he incorporated shutters and the beautiful archway in the kitchen, which I found in Italy."

Reimagined from the ground up, the characterful home oozes charm and vibrancy with its architectural elements and furnishings. Materials, textures and colors distinguish one space from the next, while vintage treasures mingle with European finds that lend French flair to every room.

PAGES 172 & 173 *Renée is an avid gardener and reaps the benefits with spectacular blooms, which she uses to create lush bouquets for every room. In appreciation for all the work she has done to restore her home, the fireplace was gifted to her. Its worn appearance elevates decay to beautiful. Small easels on the mantel display tattered tomes that pay homage to New Orleans.*

LEFT *In the living room, an oversized poster by 1920s French-Italian artist Leonetto Cappiello adds drama, along with a salvaged column, a vintage iron candelabra and a leather sofa and armchairs. Antique valances/pelmets are a perfect fit for the old windows. With a small table and chairs and a wall of glasses, an intimate corner recalls a Parisian café.*

OPPOSITE *Renée visited many historic homes in France in search of interiors inspiration for this house. In the bedroom, an architectural* oeil-de-boeuf *window frame presides over the bed, which was made by a local craftsman. Light shades of blue mingle pleasingly with deeper ones. "I do love how the salvaged flooring planks came together!" she says.*

LEFT *Renée dubbed this recessed area of the bedroom "the nostalgia corner" because it holds books and prints inherited from her parents. The weathered table displays an ever-changing array from her treasure trove of family mementoes accompanied by seasonal garden blooms.*

BELOW *Shutters lead to the narrow bathroom, which doesn't feel crowded, thanks to the high ceiling and walls and trim painted the same color. An antique French daybed, clawfoot tub and Turkish marble sink lit by chandeliers confer an old-world mood.*

Renée dubbed the house "St. Mary" for its location on the street of the same name. It has been a hub of activity ever since, especially now that the neighborhood has become very posh. "Everyone just loves the house," she says. Today, Renée makes her primary home in Southern California (see her Santa Barbara home on pages 100–111), but she sneaks away whenever she can to this charming getaway—so perfectly restored that it has been awarded a plaque by the city of New Orleans.

Renée's residence on St. Mary Street is, indeed, an ideal place to regroup with a *café au lait* and a croissant or to gather with friends in the sunny kitchen to toast Mardi-Gras with an absinthe frappé, rumored to have been a favorite drink of Mark Twain and Oscar Wilde when they visited the Crescent City. *Santé*!

ABOVE & RIGHT *A scalloped border adds cottage charm to an existing window. The kitchen cabinets were painted off-white and blue-gray to harmonize with the durable Corian countertops.*

OPPOSITE *Rachel fashioned a pair of narrow shelves from long marble slabs. A bag from the famed French bakery Poilâne in Paris is framed as art. "It's not only beautiful but very meaningful," she says. A table constructed from 2x4s and pine boards provides working space and storage with a small footprint.*

Francophile
Finesse

Like many who have been lucky enough to visit Paris, Rachel Muller returned enamored, not only with the City of Light but also with daily routines of strolling by impressive architecture and verdant parks. Today Rachel has found a way to bring the best of both worlds into the home she shares with her husband Chad and their two boys in a quiet section of St. Paul, Minnesota, where a picturesque lake and pavilion are within walking distance of their 1940s home.

"Once I find a color I love,
I will use it time and again."

As it is often the case with homes built around this time, rooms can be odd-shaped and small. "When we bought the house, we didn't think of all the things we could do to change it; we went in thinking of all the things we could do to enhance what was already there," Rachel says. "A few architectural limitations have caused us some headaches, but we love our cottage despite its quirks. It was a canvas where I could put my mark on rooms and still maintain the integrity of the original features."

While many homeowners are ready to tear down walls, Rachel grabbed her paintbrush instead and proceeded to create the transformation with a gentle and considerate approach. "For me, lighter colors are the answer. The cohesive use of similar tones and textures and plenty of light make the rooms feel spacious despite their small size." She admits to having spent a lot of time pondering a multitude of paint options before making a commitment. "Once I find a color I love, I will use it time and again, so it's worth the effort!" she explains. Throughout the home, walls are painted in watery grays and blues, producing a harmonious open flow from room to room. Keeping the main scheme pale and similar in tone allows her to introduce strokes of color with smaller accents like fabrics, trims, dishes and pillows.

Most of the furniture comes from The Porch & Atelier in nearby Buffalo, Minnesota, a second-hand furnishings and decorative paint shop owned by Rachel's mother Teresa DeJarlais. Rachel cites her mom as a major influence and the two often travel to France on shopping expeditions.

Rachel uses "blended" to describe her decorating style, which incorporates French, English Country and Swedish influences. "I think that the most personal way to decorate is to take elements from different styles and make them work together," says Rachel, who often gives pieces a paint makeover in creamy white or flax. Having so many furnishings in this palette allows her to switch pieces from room to room, a practice she does regularly to keep spaces fresh and lively. While frugal with some things, she suggests

OPPOSITE & ABOVE *Rachel wanted something different than traditional wainscoting, so she chose ceiling tiles rather than beadboard for below the chair/dado rail. To unite the table, chairs and cabinet—all second-hand finds—she painted them all white. A palette of dusty cerulean blues introduces soft color to the serene setting.*

The use of similar tones and textures gives a spacious feel to the small living room, which is filled with natural light. Fabric stretched over a canvas and framed French documents from the 1700s add subtle pattern to the walls.

ABOVE *Small homes are notorious for their lack of storage. Rachel's solution is to incorporate hutches/dressers, china cabinets and armoires like the ample one seen here. Baskets on top take advantage of the additional space. On either side, paired wall sconces and chairs provide symmetry.*

RIGHT *Rachel excels in finding a new purpose for items of varied provenance. Here, she married a wood panel and a starburst mirror into one piece with paint and distressing. She then hung it above a small cabinet to create a display and storage area (and one-of-a-kind focal point) in the living room.*

LEFT *Though small, the bathroom is big on style, with original black-and-white tiled flooring from the 1940s, beadboard walls and period fixtures. Rachel freshened up the room with white paint and clip-on shades for the wall sconces. She also ushered in a bit of color with light blue accessories that give the space an up-to-date feel yet retain its vintage charm.*

BELOW LEFT *Tucked under the rafters, a small desk offers a spot to write and also makes a convenient nightstand, keeping books, flowers and a timepiece within reach.*

RIGHT *In the long and narrow main bedroom, Rachel made space for the bed by skipping traditional nightstands. Instead, she placed a tiny shelf and wall lamp on one side and a small desk on the other. Walls are painted a watery blue that highlights the crisp linens, patterned pillows and matching shade/blind.*

quality pieces when it counts. "Pick one thing to splurge on, or if you really love an expensive piece of fabric, buy one yard of it to recover a bench or chair seat. It will have the same impact and will make you really happy every time you see it," she says.

Using objects meant for one purpose in a different way is another favorite decorating approach. Examples include kitchen shelves made from marble slabs and simple brackets, or nailing ceiling tiles to the

walls for interest. She also appreciates the period elements of her house, such as the black-and-white tiled flooring in the bathroom. Rather than switch it out for something trendy, she worked with it to preserve the vintage charm, which made her fall for the house in the first place.

A trademark of Rachel's design is strategy: she sizes up the possibilities in objects and uses them in different ways, resulting in spaces that are refined and relaxed, traditional without being staid. "I love that our home's decor is classic and understated, but when you really get to the heart of it, there is so much more beneath," she explains. "If homes reflect their owners, then I hope that is what I have accomplished with this house." Indeed, she has while also giving her home a certain *je ne sais quoi*.

Sources

SHOPS

**Beautiful Mess
Home & Garden**
Agoura Hills, CA
abeautifulmesshome.com
*Beautiful pieces for indoors and
out, curated and imported by
designer Kymberley Fraser.*

Blu Canoe
Balboa Island, CA
www.theblucanoe.com
*French-inspired preloved and
vintage home goods, bistro
style and hand-crafted items,
furnishings and decor.*

City Farmhouse
Franklin, TN
cityfarmhousefranklin.com
*One of-a-kind American and
European furniture for vintage
or new farmhouse style.*

My Favorite Room
McKinney, TX
www.kbmdesignsinteriors.com
*French imports and local finds
in a beautiful shop.*

Patine
Santa Cruz, CA
euro-linens.com
*European vintage textiles and
antique country pieces.*

The Mart Collective
Venice, CA
@themartcollective
Antique, vintage and modern.

The Porch in Buffalo
Buffalo, MN
theporchinbuffalo.com
*A premier shop offering French
and American estate finds and
vintage items.*

T. L. Gurley Antiques
Pasadena, CA
gurleyantiques.com
*A diverse inventory spanning
from ancient to modern.*

Tumbleweed & Dandelion
Venice, CA
tumbleweedanddandelion.com
*From art to textiles kitchen
goods, dishware and more, Lizzie
McGraw's iconic shop offers
unique items acquired from
French flea markets.*

Vignettes
San Diego, CA
vignettesantiques.com
*Exclusive vintage home decor with
an emphasis on French country,
rustic and architectural elements.*

ANTIQUES MARKETS, SHOWS & AUCTIONS

Atelier de Campagne
Watsonville, CA
@atelierdecampagne
*All things French for the home
and garden.*

**Brimfield Antique
Flea Markets**
Brimfield, MA
brimfieldantiquefleamarket.com
*One of the most attended shows,
with an abundance of exclusive
French and European antiques.*

Rose Bowl Flea Market
Pasadena, CA
rgcshows.com/rose-bowl
*Known all over the world for its
unique array of high-quality items,
this market takes place on the
second Sunday of each month.*

Santa Barbara Antique Show
Santa Barbara, CA
sbantiqueshow.com
*Held twice a year, this show brings
the finest antiques and vintage
dealers to Santa Barbara.*

**Santa Monica Antique
and Vintage Market**
Santa Monica, CA
santamonicaairport
    antiquemarket.com
*A twice-monthly destination
for decorators, designers and
boutique owners as well as
the general public.*

**The Original Round
Top Antiques Fair**
Round Top and Warrenton, TX
roundtoptexasantiques.com
*Featuring authentic antiques from
all over the world, this triannual
show is one of the largest and
most famous in the US.*

ONLINE

1stDibs
1stdibs.com
*Since 2000, the leading online
marketplace for extraordinary
design has captured the magic
of a Parisian flea market.*

About Time Antiques
abouttimeantiques.com
*The place for online auctions
of vintage items, collectibles
and home decor.*

Baumalu
gourmet-web.com/Baumalu_1
*French manufacturer of copper
cookware, produced in the
traditional way and available
to buy from Gourmet Web.*

Bonjour le Lin
bonjourlelin.com
*Handcrafted house linens made
in Portugal from 100% pure flax
of French origin.*

Chairish
chairish.com
*A unique, curated inventory of the
most exceptional items available
in the US and Europe.*

Collected by Schwung
collectedby.schwung.design
*Unique, useful, whimsical and
beautiful pieces.*

Debra Hall Lifestyle
debrahalllifestyle.com
*Globally sourced curated
homewares and vintage finds.*

deVol Kitchens
devolkitchens.com
*Acclaimed manufacturer of bespoke
kitchens and home accessories, all
designed and made in the UK.*

Eloquence
eloquence.com
*Refined interpretations of the
finest antique furniture.*

Etsy
etsy.com
*Plaques, signs, ephemera and
furniture—search for key phrases
such as 'authentic French antique'
to find the best items.*

French Broc'
etsy.com/shop/
FrenchBrocBoutique
*Smaller decorative items straight
from France's brocantes.*

Gina Bowhill
ginabowhill.com
*European antiques and heritage
pieces for the home.*

ILVE
us.ilve.com
*From the appeal of classic styles
to new design trends, ILVE kitchen
appliances share a timeless beauty.*

Perigold
perigold.com
*Offers a wide selection of
unique pieces with meticulous
craftsmanship.*

Preservation Station
thepreservationstation.com
*Antique lighting and unusual
architectural elements.*

Rachel Ashwell Shabby Chic
shabbychic.com
*Since 1989, Rachel Ashwell's
eponymous brand has been your
source for beautiful heirloom
pieces that combine all the best of
modern style and classic charm.*

The French Farmer's Wife
facebook.com/
TheFrenchFarmersWifeNC
*A curated collection of antique
and vintage European furniture
for the home and garden.*

Picture Credits

All photography by Mark Lohman.
Key: a = above; b = below; l = left; c = center; r = right.

Page 1 The home of Angela Mann in Los Angeles; 2 The home of Kathy and Doug McCabe in McKinney, Texas; 3 The home of Laurence and Christophe Gomez in Tarzana, California; 4 The home of Sandra and Jeff Linderman in Thousand Oaks, California; 5 a The home of Penelope and Adam Bianchi in Montecito, California; 5 b The home of Renée Parker in Santa Barbara, California; 6 The home of Kathy and Doug McCabe in McKinney, Texas; 7 The home of Angela Mann in Los Angeles; 8–9 The home of Chantal Cloutier in Solvang, California; 10 The home of Andalynn and Brandon Richie in Southern California; 11 a The home of Kathy and Doug McCabe in McKinney, Texas; 11 b The home of Angela Mann in Los Angeles; 12 al & bl The home of Sandra and Jeff Linderman in Thousand Oaks, California; 12 ar The home of Chantal Cloutier in Solvang, California; 13 The home of Sandra and Jeff Linderman in Thousand Oaks, California; 14 The home of Chantal Cloutier in Solvang, California; 15 The home of Andalynn and Brandon Richie in Southern California; 16 l The home of Chantal Cloutier in Solvang, California; 16 ar & br The home of Andalynn and Brandon Richie in Southern California; 17 The home of Sandra and Jeff Linderman in Thousand Oaks, California; 18 The home of Andalynn and Brandon Richie in Southern California; 19 l The home of Kathy and Doug McCabe in McKinney, Texas; 19 ar The home of Renée Parker in Santa Barbara, California; 19 br The home of Chantal Cloutier in Solvang, California; 20 The home of Charley and Kathee Zurian in Kernersville, North Carolina; 21 al & ar The home of Sandra and Jeff Linderman in Thousand Oaks, California; 21 cl The home of Charley and Kathee Zurian in Kernersville, North Carolina; 21 cr The home of Laurence and Christophe Gomez in Tarzana, California; 21 bl & br The home of Renée Parker in Santa Barbara, California; 22 The home of Sandra and Jeff Linderman in Thousand Oaks, California; 23 al The home of Laurence and Christophe Gomez in Tarzana, California; 23 ar The home of Rachel and Chad Muller in St. Paul, Minnesota 23 b The home of Sue and Tim Johnson in Phoenix, Arizona; 24 The home of Charley and Kathee Zurian in Kernersville, North Carolina; 25 al & ar The home of Laurence and Christophe Gomez in Tarzana, California; 25 cl The home of Chantal Cloutier in Solvang, California; 25 cr The home of Rachel and Chad Muller in St. Paul, Minnesota 25 br The home of Angela Mann in Los Angeles; 26 The home of Chantal Cloutier in Solvang, California; 27 al The home of Renée Parker in Santa Barbara, California; 27 br The home of Angela Mann in Los Angeles; 28 The home of Laurence and Christophe Gomez in Tarzana, California; 29 al The home of Rachel and Chad Muller in St. Paul, Minnesota 29 ar The home of Penelope and Adam Bianchi in Montecito, California; 29 cl The home of Sue and Tim Johnson in Phoenix, Arizona; 29 cr The home of Rachel and Chad Muller in St. Paul, Minnesota 29 bl The home of Kathy and Doug McCabe in McKinney, Texas; 29 br & 30 The home of Laurence and Christophe Gomez in Tarzana, California; 31 al The home of Penelope and Adam Bianchi in Montecito, California; 31 bl The home of Renée Parker in New Orleans; 31 br The home of Kathy and Doug McCabe in McKinney, Texas; 32 The home of Andalynn and Brandon Richie in Southern California; 33 The home of Angela Mann in Los Angeles; 34 The home of Sandra and Jeff Linderman in Thousand Oaks, California; 35 al & r The home of Laurence and Christophe Gomez in Tarzana, California; 35 bl The home of Sue and Tim Johnson in Phoenix, Arizona; 36 al The home of Penelope and Adam Bianchi in Montecito, California; 36 ar The home of Sue and Tim Johnson in Phoenix, Arizona; 36 b The home of Renée Parker in Santa Barbara, California; 37 The home of Angela Mann in Los Angeles; 38 The home of Laurence and Christophe Gomez in Tarzana, California; 39 The home of Sandra and Jeff Linderman in Thousand Oaks, California; 40 a The home of Laurence and Christophe Gomez in Tarzana, California; 40 b The home of Kathy and Doug McCabe in McKinney, Texas; 41 The home of Andalynn and Brandon Richie in Southern California; 42 The home of Penelope and Adam Bianchi in Montecito, California; 43 The home of Andalynn and Brandon Richie in Southern California; 44 al & bl The home of Laurence and Christophe Gomez in Tarzana, California; 44 br The home of Angela Mann in Los Angeles; 45 The home of Laurence and Christophe Gomez in Tarzana, California; 48–63 The home of Andalynn and Brandon Richie in Southern California; 64–75 The home of Angela Mann in Los Angeles; 76–87 The home of Sandra and Jeff Linderman in Thousand Oaks, California; 88–99 The home of Kathy and Doug McCabe in McKinney, Texas; 100–111 The home of Renée Parker in Santa Barbara, California; 112–121 The home of Penelope and Adam Bianchi in Montecito, California; 122–135 The home of Laurence and Christophe Gomez n Tarzana, California; 136–145 The home of Chantal Cloutier in Solvang, California; 146–155 The home of Sue and Tim Johnson in Phoenix, Arizona; 156–169 The home of Charley and Kathee Zurian in Kernersville, North Carolina; 170–177 The home of Renée Parker in New Orleans; 178–185 The home of Rachel and Chad Muller in St. Paul, Minnesota; 186 The home of Sue and Tim Johnson in Phoenix, Arizona; 192 l The home of Penelope and Adam Bianchi in Montecito, California; 192 c & r The home of Renée Parker in Santa Barbara, California.

Business Credits

Key: a = above; b = below; l = left; c = center; r = right.

Andalynn Richie
Architectural, interior, equestrian and garden designer

Maison du Cheval Bleu
maisonduchevalbleu.com
IG: @maisonduchevalbleu

Pages 10, 15, 16 ar & br, 18, 32, 41, 43, 48–63

Sandra Linderman
Designer and antiques dealer

The Mart Collective
IG: @themartcollective

Summerland Antique Collective
www.summerlandantiquecollective.com

Pages 4, 12 al & bl, 13, 17, 21 al & ar, 22, 34, 39, 76–87

Kathy McCabe
Interior designer

KBM Designs Interiors
www.kbmdesignsinteriors.com

Pages 2, 6, 11 a, 19 l, 29 bl, 31 br, 40 b, 88–99

Penelope Bianchi
Interior designer

McCormick Interiors
mccormickinteriors.com

Pages 5 a, 29 ar, 31 al, 36 al, 42, 112–121, 192 l

Laurence Gomez
Antiques dealer

French Broc'
etsy.com/shop/FrenchBrocBoutique

Pages 3, 21 cr, 23 al, 25 al & ar, 28, 29 br, 30, 35 al & r, 38, 40 a, 44 al & bl, 45, 122–135

Chantal Cloutier

Brendan McBreen Designs
Interior designer
Phone: +1 310 309-7177
Email: brendanjmcbreen@gmail.com

Pages 8–9, 12 ar, 14, 16 l, 19 br, 25 cl, 26, 136–145

Kathee Zurian
Antiques dealer

The French Farmer's Wife
facebook.com/TheFrenchFarmersWifeNC

Pages 20, 21 cl, 24, 156–169

Index

Acknowledgments

If you are lucky, once in a long time life hands you a gift. In my case, this happened in 2010 when David Peters took a chance on publishing my first book. I am forever beholden. With every book, past and present, David's legacy lives on.

I have met with more support than ever from countless people from everywhere, including each of the homeowners featured in this book. My heartfelt thanks to Laurence and Christophe Gomez, Sandra and Jeff Linderman, Angela Mann, Penelope and Adam Bianchi, Chantal Cloutier, Andalynn and Brandon Richie, Sue and Tim Johnson, Renee Parker, Kathy McCabe, Rachel and Chad Muller and Kathee and Charley Zurian. Your kindness feeds my soul.

Many many thanks to the creative team at Ryland Peters & Small and CICO Books for enabling me to keep creating books year after year: Annabel Morgan, senior commissioning editor; Sophie Devlin, editor; Toni Kay, senior designer; Sally Powell, art director, Leslie Harrington, creative director and Gordana Simakovic, production manager. I carry you all in my heart.

I am as honored today as I was 15 years ago to be a small part of such a genuinely nurturing company and fortunate to still be working with Mark Lohman whose beautiful photographs make every book that much more special. Thank you, Mark.

With much love to all,
Fifi